New Thinking in Soviet Politics

Edited by

Archie Brown
Professor of Politics
University of Oxford

Palgrave Macmillan

ISBN 978-0-333-53440-3   ISBN 978-1-349-21897-4 (eBook)
DOI 10.1007/978-1-349-21897-4

First published in the United States of America in 1992
ISBN 978-0-312-07919-2

Library of Congress Cataloging-in-Publication Data
New thinking in Soviet politics / edited by Archie Brown.
p.   cm.
Includes index.
ISBN 978-0-312-07919-2
1. Soviet Union—Politics and government—1985-   2. Soviet Union-
-Economic conditions—1985-   I. Brown, Archie, 1929-   .
JN6581.N48   1992
320.947'09'048—dc20   91–43095
                                                          CIP

NEW THINKING IN SOVIET POLITICS

Contents

Preface   vii

Notes on the Contributors   ix

1   Introduction
     Archie Brown   1

2   New Thinking on the Soviet Political System
     Archie Brown   12

3   New Thinking on the Soviet Economy
     Alec Nove   29

4   New Thinking and the National Question
     Gail W. Lapidus   39

5   New Thinking in Soviet Foreign Policy
     Alexander Dallin   71

6   New Thinking about World Communism
     Alexander Dallin   86

7   Some Concluding Observations
     T. H. Rigby   102

Index   111

Preface

This book is an outgrowth of a panel discussion on 'New Thinking in Soviet Politics' which I convened at the Fourth World Congress for Soviet and East European Studies, held at Harrogate, in July 1990. From the outset it was intended to be a coherent book and not merely a collection of papers. The volume – while remaining concise – is, accordingly, a good deal more comprehensive than the panel could be, limited as the latter was to three papers by eminently sensible Congress rules designed to allow time for contributions from the floor.

My first debt of gratitude is, though, to those who participated in the Congress panel: the two paper-givers, Alexander Dallin and Alec Nove (I was the author of the third), T. H. Rigby who chaired the session, and Alex Pravda who acted as discussant for all three papers. Alec Nove's paper, with some updating, remains closest of all the chapters in the book to the Harrogate version. Alex Dallin was kind enough to accept my suggestion that his Harrogate paper be turned into two chapters – one on 'New Thinking in Soviet Foreign Policy' and the other on 'New Thinking about World Communism'. My gratitude to him for doing so will, I am sure, be shared by readers of this volume.

In addition to my Introduction, there are also two other chapters which were not among the three papers in the Harrogate 'New Thinking' panel. One is by Gail Lapidus who, in another part of the Harrogate programme, was exploring the same issue – the development of new ideas in Soviet politics – in the context of discussion of the National Question. I am extremely grateful to her for turning her paper into a chapter for this book, covering that crucial area of recent and contemporary Soviet politics. Harry Rigby, having been an excellent chairman of the Congress panel (which attracted wide interest and a large audience), has put me further in his debt by contributing a chapter of concluding reflections.

My own work for the book benefited from a Personal Research Grant from the Economic and Social Research Council of the UK for the study of Soviet political debates and from visits to the Soviet Union made possible by the British Academy. I am most grateful to both of those bodies. I am also, and not for the first time, greatly indebted to my wife, Pat, for compiling the index to this volume.

On the vexed issue of transliteration, I have followed the British Standard system (which is used also by many American publications), but with a few simplifications, such as the 'sky' endings in proper names and the use of *perestroika* rather than *perestroyka* in the text on the grounds that, with the former spelling, the word has virtually entered the English language. (The latter spelling – which corresponds strictly to the transliteration system adopted – is reserved for the occurrence of the word in the titles of Russian books listed in the end-notes.)

This volume was conceived and begun in St Antony's College, Oxford, and completed in Austin, Texas, where I have been spending the 1990–1 academic year as a Visiting Professor in the Department of Government. Both Oxford, to which I shall have returned by the time the book appears, and Austin have been in their different ways splendidly supportive academic environments. The research underpinnings provided by the University of Texas at Austin and the outstanding library resources of Oxford University in the Soviet field have made their contribution to such merits as this collective volume may possess.

My final debt is to the book's British and American publishers and, in particular, to Tim Farmiloe for combining enthusiasm, experience and efficiency with patience.

Archie Brown
Austin, Texas: 1991

Notes on the Contributors

Archie Brown has been a Fellow of St Antony's College, Oxford, since 1971 and Professor of Politics at Oxford University since 1989. Earlier he was Lecturer in Politics at Glasgow University (1964–71) and Lecturer in Soviet Institutions at Oxford (1971–89). He has been a Visiting Professor at Yale University; the University of Connecticut; Columbia University, New York; and most recently, in 1990–1, at the University of Texas at Austin (as holder of the Frank C. Erwin, Jr. Centennial Chair in Government). He was elected a Fellow of the British Academy in 1991. Professor Brown gave the Henry L. Stimson Lectures at Yale in 1980, the annual lectures of the Stanford University Center for Russian and East European Studies in 1988 and the Arnold Wolfers Visiting Fellow Lecture for 1989 at Yale.

He is the author of *Soviet Politics and Political Science* (1974; US edition, 1976) and *The Gorbachev Factor in Soviet Politics* (1992) and the editor of (and contributor to) *The Soviet Union since the Fall of Khrushchev* (with Michael Kaser, 1975; US edition, 1976; 2nd edn, 1978), *Political Culture and Political Change in Communist States* (with Jack Gray, 1977; 2nd edn, 1979), *Authority, Power and Policy in the USSR* (with T. H. Rigby and Peter Reddaway, 1980), *The Cambridge Encyclopedia of Russia and the Soviet Union* (with John Fennell, Michael Kaser and H. T. Willetts, 1982; 2nd edn, with Michael Kaser and Gerald S. Smith, 1992), *Political Culture and Communist Studies* (1984; US edition, 1985), *Political Leadership in the Soviet Union* (1989) and *The Soviet Union: A Biographical Dictionary* (1990; US edition, 1991).

Alexander Dallin is Raymond A. Spruance Professor of International History and Professor of Political Science at Stanford University. Before moving to Stanford in 1971, he was Adlai A. Stevenson Professor of International Relations at Columbia University (1965–71) and Director of Columbia's Russian Institute (1962–7). A former President of the American Association for the Advancement of Slavic Studies (1984–5) and President of the International Council for Soviet and East European Studies (1985–90), he served as Director of Stanford's Center for Russian and East European Studies (1985–9) and as Phi Beta Kappa Lecturer (1989–90).

Professor Dallin is the author of numerous publications on Soviet affairs and international relations. His books include *German Rule in Russia* (1957; rev. edn, 1981), *The Soviet Union at the United Nations* (1962), *The Soviet Union and Disarmament* (1965), *Political Terror in Communist Systems* (1970), and *Black Box: KAL 007 and the Superpowers* (1985). He is the editor or co-editor of (and contributor to) *Soviet Conduct in World Affairs* (1960; 2nd edn, 1975), *Politics in the Soviet Union: Seven Cases* (with Alan F. Westin, 1966), *Soviet Politics since Khrushchev* (with Thomas B. Larson, 1968), *Women in Russia* (with Dorothy Atkinson and Gail W. Lapidus, 1977), *The Gorbachev Era* (with Condoleeza Rice, 1986), *U.S.–Soviet Security Cooperation* (with Alexander George and Philip Farley, 1988), *Soviet Scholarship under Gorbachev* (with Bertrand Patenaude, 1988) and *The Soviet Union in Crisis* (with Gail Lapidus, 1991).

Gail W. Lapidus received her Ph.D. from Harvard University in 1974 and has been a Professor of Political Science at the University of California at Berkeley since 1976 and the Chair of the Berkeley–Stanford Programme in Soviet Studies since 1985. She was a Fellow of the Woodrow Wilson International Center for Scholars in 1982–3, a Senior Fellow of the W. Averell Harriman Institute for Advanced Study of the USSR at Columbia University in 1983–4 and, most recently (1986–7), a Fellow at the Center for Advanced Study in the Behavioral Sciences. A specialist on Soviet politics and foreign policy, she is a member of the Council on Foreign Relations, for whom she directed the 1985–6 Study Group on Soviet–American Relations.

Professor Lapidus is the author of *Women in Soviet Society* (1978) which is currently being revised for publication in the Soviet Union, and co-editor of *Women in Russia* (with Dorothy Atkinson and Alexander Dallin, 1977), *The Glasnost Papers: Voices on Reform from Moscow* (with Andrei Melville, 1990) and *The Soviet Union in Crisis* (with Alexander Dallin, 1991). A frequent visitor to the USSR, Professor Lapidus is currently working on a book on nationalism and the Soviet future.

Alec Nove was Professor of Economics and Director of the Institute of Soviet and East European Studies at Glasgow University from 1963 until his retirement in 1982. Before that, from 1947 until 1958, he was a civil servant (mainly at the Board of Trade) and from 1958 to 1963 he was Reader in Russian Social and Economic Studies at the

University of London. He is currently Professor Emeritus and Honorary Senior Research Fellow of Glasgow University. A Fellow of the British Academy since 1978, he is also a Fellow of the Royal Society of Edinburgh and an Honorary Fellow of the London School of Economics and Political Science. He has been a Visiting Professor or Visiting Scholar at the Universities of Kansas; Pennsylvania; Columbia (twice); Moscow; Santiago, Chile; Paris; Rennes; U.C.L.A. and most recently, in 1990, at Harvard and at the Stockholm School of Economics.

Professor Nove's numerous books include *The Soviet Economy* (1961), *Was Stalin Really Necessary?* (1964), *The Soviet Middle East* (with J. A. Newth, 1965), *An Economic History of the USSR* (1969), *Socialist Economics* (co-editor with D. M. Nuti, 1972), *Efficiency Criteria for Nationalised Industries* (1973), *Stalinism and After* (1975; 3rd edn, 1989), *The Soviet Economic System* (1977; 3rd edn, 1987), *Political Economy and Soviet Socialism* (1978), *Socialism, Economics and Development* (1986), *Glasnost in Action: Cultural Renaissance in Russia* (1989), *Studies in Economics and Russia* (1990) and *Economics of Feasible Socialism Revisited* (1991).

T. H. Rigby has been Professorial Fellow and later Professor of Political Science in the Research School of Social Sciences of the Australian National University, Canberra, since 1964. A graduate of Melbourne University, he received his doctorate from the University of London. His early career included wartime service in the Australian army, work in the British Foreign Office and British Embassy in Moscow, teaching Russian language and literature in Melbourne and Canberra, and collaborative research with Leonard Schapiro at the London School of Economics and Political Science. Professor Rigby has held visiting appointments at St Antony's College, Oxford, the Kennan Institute of Advanced Russian Studies in Washington, DC, the Academy of Sciences of the USSR, and Columbia, Moscow and Cologne Universities.

He is the author of *Communist Party Membership in the USSR 1917–1967* (1968), *Lenin's Government* (1979), *Political Elites in the USSR* (1990) and *The Changing Soviet System* (1990). He is also the editor of (and contributor to) *Stalin* (1965), *The Disintegrating Monolith: Pluralist Trends in the Communist World* (1965), *Authority, Power and Policy in the USSR* (with Archie Brown and Peter Reddaway, 1980), *Political Legitimation in Communist States* (with

Ferenc Feher, 1982), *Leadership Selection and Patron–Client Relations in the USSR and Yugoslavia* (with Bohdan Harasymiw, 1983) and *Gorbachev at the Helm: A New Era in Soviet Politics?* (with R. F. Miller and J. H. Miller, 1987).

1 Introduction
Archie Brown

The term, 'New Thinking' (or 'New Political Thinking') was used in the Soviet Union in 1986–7 mainly with reference to foreign policy. Mikhail Gorbachev's book, *Perestroika: New Thinking for Our Country and the World*,[1] published in 1987, was somewhat ambiguous in this respect. Its sub-title suggested that 'New Thinking' embraced both the domestic and international scene, but the organization of the book did not fully bear this out. It was divided into two parts. The first was entitled 'Perestroika' and was concerned with Soviet internal developments and aspirations and the second – termed 'New Thinking and the World' – was devoted to foreign affairs. However, from 1988 onwards 'New Thinking' – in authoritative Soviet statements – increasingly came to embrace the conceptual revolution which has been underway in the sphere of domestic politics as well as in foreign policy. Thus, for example, a collection of Fedor Burlatsky's articles and plays published in 1989 under the title *New Thinking* is subtitled 'Dialogues and opinions on the technological revolution and our reforms'[2] and is devoted mainly to Soviet domestic politics, even though Burlatsky has been a contributor to the new thinking on foreign policy as well.

The scope and significance of the term, 'New Political Thinking', in official Soviet discourse is not entirely easy to pin down, partly because the meaning of 'official' or 'authoritative' Soviet pronouncements has itself become far less clear. Even in Brezhnev's time it was a gross oversimplification to assume that every article in a Soviet newspaper represented a single 'official' view, for there was some cautiously expressed divergence of opinion. But books, journals and newspapers prior to the Gorbachev era reflected to a much greater extent than they did in the late 1980s the range of views Soviet officialdom deemed permissible for mass dissemination. There were, of course, some exceptions, as when individual authors, with or without the connivance of their editors, managed to say something radically unorthodox between the lines.

By the end of the 1980s there was little need for such deviousness. A number of editors had taken to acting independently and many views and analyses were published which went well beyond what was

1

regarded as desirable by the country's top political leadership, although it is difficult to generalize about the views of the latter since they were so deeply divided. What was perfectly acceptable to Aleksandr Yakovlev was frequently unacceptable to Yegor Ligachev – with Gorbachev's views usually much closer to those of Yakovlev than to the positions of Ligachev. At any rate, the boundaries of *glasnost'* continued to expand up to April 1991 (the cut-off point of this book), even though the backlash against those publications which had been most forthright in their dismissal of outmoded dogma had also become more powerful. So great was the expansion that keeping up with the flow of publications of previously taboo books and articles and of controversial new works became well-nigh impossible for even the most assiduous of individual scholars, although some valuable individual and collective efforts have been made.[3]

The picture of officially-countenanced 'New Thinking' was complicated by the fact that by 1990 there was a multiplicity of conflicting authorities in the Soviet Union. One result of the new political practice which followed the new political thinking was competitive elections for a legislature representing the entire USSR in 1989 and elections for the legislatures of the fifteen Union republics in 1990. The latter produced non-communist and nationalist majorities in several republics and even in the case of the giant Russian republic a Supreme Soviet, under the chairmanship of Boris Yel'tsin, which was frequently at odds with the Supreme Soviet of the USSR. The outcome was termed *mnogovlastie* ('many powers' or 'a multiplicity of powers') by, among others, the leading Soviet constitutional lawyer and Chairman of the Committee for Supervision of the Constitution, Sergey Alekseev.[4] Republican governments and legislatures began to adopt very different policies and their relations with the mass media also varied greatly. The Russian republic alone saw the birth of many new newspapers, including at the national level, *Rossiyskaya gazeta* (the newspaper of the Supreme Soviet of the Russian republic), *Rossiya* (the organ of the Presidium of the Supreme Soviet of the RSFSR) and the increasingly popular and interesting *Nezavisimaya gazeta* (*Independent Newspaper*).

In the chapters that follow, the contributors to this volume concentrate their attention on that new thinking which has found its way into mass circulation newspapers and books and, still more, on the new ideas which have been accepted by Soviet policymakers, especially at the all-Union level, even though in terms of sheer radicalism one could find views which diverge still further from traditional

Soviet norms in several of the republics. An examination of contemporary political thought in the Soviet republics would, however, call for a separate and larger study. At the same time the emphasis is on *new ideas* of political consequence and not only on what Soviet leaders or officials have included within the canon of New Political Thinking. To the extent that the latter concept can degenerate into a slogan, its importance might be questioned, but no serious student of politics could question the significance of genuinely new concepts in the Soviet context entering the political vocabulary and consciousness of both leaders and peoples. Language, as James Farr has observed, is 'an arena of political action' and 'where there are different concepts, there are different beliefs, and so different actions and practices'.[5]

The roots of the new thinking are diverse. Some of them can be traced to a re-evaluation of pre-revolutionary and non-Soviet Russian thinking. Thus, for example, such a mainstream reformer as Mikhail Piskotin, the chief editor of the journal, *Narodnyy deputat*, noted in the course of a fascinating article entitled 'To call things by their proper names' which appeared in the pages of his journal in 1990, that not until that year had Nikolay Berdyaev's book, *The Origins and Idea of Russian Communism* (for long 'widely known in the whole world') been published in the Soviet Union.[6] Piskotin reflects on the impoverishment of intellectual life that resulted when such 'brilliant minds' as Berdyaev were lost to the country.[7] The *émigré* Russian philosopher, Berdyaev, had a clandestine following among Russian intellectuals as far back as Brezhnev's time, but it is only within the last few years that it has been possible for his work to be praised in the pages of the official journal of the Supreme Soviet.

Other roots of the new thinking are to be found in Soviet scholars' gradual acquaintanceship with Western social science literature which began to take place under Khrushchev and went further under Brezhnev, even though it was only dimly reflected in Soviet published works of that period. Soviet dissident writing of the Brezhnev years (not least the ideas – and example – of Andrey Sakharov) can also be seen as one of the sources of even the official New Political Thinking of the Gorbachev era.

By 1990 and early 1991, a realignment had taken place in Soviet politics and many former within-system reformers were espousing views no different from the most radical pronouncements of the former dissidents. The dividing line between the views of the latter and the communists or former communists who constitute a majority of the leading figures in the political opposition in Russia became an exceedingly fine one. Such leaders as Gavriil Popov (the Chairman of the Moscow City Soviet), Anatoliy Sobchak (Chairman of the Leningrad City Soviet), Yuriy Afanas'ev (the Director of the Moscow State Historical Archival Institute) and, of course, the former full-time party functionary, Boris Yel'tsin, all of whom resigned from the Communist Party as recently as 1990, had by that year made public pronouncements which had more in common with the views of former dissidents (some of whom are now part of the same broad 'Democratic Russia' movement) than with the ideology to which they publicly subscribed in the past.

The Soviet domestic political scene is in a state of flux and the outcome of the various political struggles has become extremely difficult to predict. Up to the present, however, the beliefs and decisions of the all-Union political authorities (those of Gorbachev and of the key institutional actors in the leadership at the level of the USSR) have a special importance for outside analysts. That is most clearly so in the case of foreign policy where the key players have been Gorbachev himself, the Ministry of Foreign Affairs (especially under Eduard Shevardnadze's leadership from July 1985 until December 1990), the Central Committee apparatus of the Soviet Communist Party and (particularly since 1990) the military and the KGB. Even in domestic politics, though the republics have acquired sufficient *de facto* power to frustrate the wishes of the central authorities, what is decided at the all-Union level is (as of early 1991) likely to affect more people's lives in the Soviet Union than decisions taken at any of the other levels of the Soviet political system.

NEW THINKING AND THE POWER STRUCTURE

Hence, attention is devoted in this book not simply to all new thinking on politics which has ever taken place in the Soviet Union, for that could be located in small groups both of overt dissidents and of discreet within-system reformers prior to Gorbachev's accession to the General Secretaryship of the Soviet Communist Party, but to the new thinking which has penetrated the highest echelons of the Soviet power structure, especially in the years 1987–90. One could make a case for saying that this was the decisive period for the development and consolidation of the New Political Thinking as a partly codified body of ideas. After the elections which took place in the various

Soviet republics in 1990, the country was in a sense *beyond* the New Thinking, understood as official doctrine, although 'new thinking' in the everyday sense of those words remained as necessary as ever and, indeed, increasingly prevalent at many different levels of society. The new legislatures produced great political differences from one republic to another and made obsolete the notion of a commonly agreed new political doctrine. The Soviet Union had moved beyond the New Thinking also inasmuch as fewer and fewer people were prepared to wait for ideas to be given an official imprimator before feeling free not only to adopt them but to espouse them publicly. Furthermore, the New Thinking had come under attack from both ends of the Soviet political spectrum.

Among the key components of the New Political Thinking elaborated between 1987 and 1990 were the idea that universal values should take precedence over a 'class approach' to international relations, that each country should be free to make its own choice of political and economic system, that cooperation take the place of conflict in an increasingly interdependent world, that in the Soviet Union itself highly authoritarian one-party rule be ended through the creation of institutions sustaining political pluralism, that support be given to the development both of a civil society and a state based upon the rule of law, that a command economy with virtually one hundred per cent state or public ownership of the means of production should be replaced by a market economy with a substantial private sector, and that an ideology and system increasingly referred to as 'totalitarian' should give way to a 'humane and democratic socialism'.[8]

While not a comprehensive account of the content of the officially-sanctioned New Thinking, such a summary of it is sufficient to show just how radical a departure from previous Soviet doctrine it represented for anyone familiar with the latter. It has, not surprisingly, come under attack from conservative communists and from officials worried about its very practical political consequences. Thus, Ivan Poloz'kov, the First Secretary of the Central Committee of the Russian Communist Party (an office and Central Committee created in the summer of 1990), has attacked most of the principal tenets of the New Thinking, including what he calls the 'anarchy of the spontaneous market'[9] and the idea that 'all-human interests', or universal values, take precedence over 'the class principle'.[10]

Yegor Ligachev, both before and after his departure from the leadership of the Soviet Communist Party in the summer of 1990, criticized the same aspects of the New Thinking and blamed the adoption of 'mistaken principles' for 'serious miscalculations in politics'. He has objected strenuously to the 'virtual abandonment' of a 'class approach' and also to the concept of socialism as a definite (and Leninist) type of social system being replaced by a much more vague attachment to 'the socialist idea'.[11] Aleksey Il'in, the second secretary of the Russian Communist Party, argued in December 1990 that the debate on the draft Union Treaty which was developing was one between supporters and opponents of 'the socialist choice' and he blamed the pre-Twenty-Eighth Party Congress Politburo and Central Committee and 'to a certain extent also the present' Politburo and Central Committee of the Soviet Communist Party for their inability to appraise these political phenomena – a product, he held, of their abandonment of a class analysis.[12]

From the other end of the political spectrum 'the socialist idea' is also being criticized either implicitly or explicitly by radical democrats and marketeers who in many cases have ceased to regard themselves as socialists. Whereas many of the social scientists among them as recently as 1988 saw the theoretical task with which they were confronted as being 'the ideological renewal of socialism',[13] comparatively few among those who belong to the broad 'Democratic Russia' grouping are any longer interested in viewing the New Thinking as the creative and open-minded development of Marxism or as the theoretical updating of the principles of socialism. If the 'New Thinking', as elaborated by Gorbachev[14] or Yakovlev,[15] represents something of a revival of the idea of 'The Third Way',[16] the increasing reluctance to subscribe to it on the part of the radical democrats reflects the abandonment of the belief many of them previously held in a new and fundamentally different type of political and economic system superior both to communist authoritarianism and its inefficient command economy, on the one hand, and to the 'bourgeois democracy' and capitalist economic order of North America and Western Europe, on the other.

The proclaimed 'democratic socialist' destination of the voyage of *perestroika* has come under increasing attack both from conservative communists and from radical liberals and democrats. It has been viewed by the conservatives as a retreat from Marxism-Leninism (as indeed it was, even when all due allowance is made for the elasticity of that term) and has been seen as posing a very real threat to the institutional interests of the Party, the ministerial bureaucracy, the military and the KGB. For many of the liberals it has represented but a stage on an intellectual journey. A number of the Soviet Union's most prominent intellectuals have followed a path which has led from orthodox communism through revisionist Marxism to democratic socialism and on to their present attachment to democratic capitalism. For Marxist-Leninist fundamentalists this, of course, is merely confirmation that even to begin to question received dogma is to take the first step down a slippery slope that leads all the way to the 'enemy camp'.

THE STIMULUS OF FAILURE

While a distinction can be made between the actual elaboration and dissemination of new ideas in the Soviet Union and the officially approved 'New Thinking', there is, of course, a substantial overlap between the two. Even the authoritative New Thinking is a far from static body of doctrine. By the time Gorbachev had embraced in principle in 1990 'political pluralism', a 'market economy' and, so far as property ownership is concerned, a 'mixed economy', he had brought official theory to the point where new Soviet *aspirations* were not so very different from West European *realities*. Whether this was ultimately to be called 'democratic socialism' or 'democratic capitalism' was not necessarily of decisive importance, except to ideologues.

In a number of areas *failure* has provided the strongest impetus to new thinking. That is clearly true in the case of the Soviet economy, the subject of Chapter 3 of this book. Its author, Alec Nove, has over many years been an exceptionally acute analyst of the workings and problems of the Soviet economic system and he is able here, in a concise account, to provide an overview and assessment of the wide range of critiques now being advanced by Soviet scholars and political activists.

The dangerous growth of inter-ethnic tensions, and the refusal over many years to come to terms with the national problem, can equally be seen, as Gail Lapidus shows in Chapter 4, as failures which were major stimuli to such new thinking as has taken place on the nationality issue within the Soviet Union. As Lapidus convincingly argues, inter-ethnic and inter-republican relations did not have a high place on the political agenda when Gorbachev succeeded Chernenko as Soviet leader. The radical reassessment of these relations in more recent years is a direct consequence of latent discontents becoming all too clearly manifest – on the one hand, in the form of demands for separate statehood on the part of at least six nationalities and, on the other, by outbreaks of inter-ethnic violence. Such new thinking as has occurred on the kind of political arrangements required to achieve a reasonable harmony within a Soviet multinational state resting on different foundations is, accordingly, as Lapidus suggests, largely a response to unintended consequences of *perestroika* and *glasnost'*.

It is not difficult to find evidence of failure also in the working of the unreformed Soviet political system, in the Soviet Union's previously adversarial relations with the non-communist world and even in its relations with other communist states. Yet, as is suggested in Chapter 2 (Brown) and in Chapters 5 and 6 (Alexander Dallin) new thinking on the Soviet polity and on the country's relations with the outside world was a conscious and deliberate undertaking on the part both of intellectual advisers of an innovative turn of mind and of the reformist wing of the Communist Party leadership itself – Gorbachev, Yakovlev and Shevardnadze – from quite early in the Gorbachev era. In due course the thinking, and its political consequences, became more radical than its initiators could have foreseen at the outset, but the pages that follow give some indication of the dramatic impact of fresh ideas on a system which had seemed to many of its critics almost irredeemably stagnant as recently as a decade ago. Indeed, the 'era of stagnation' became the most favoured sobriquet for the Brezhnev years in the lexicon of the New Thinking.

Turning upside down cherished concepts – and challenging the conventional wisdom of the *apparatchiki* – has introduced great stresses and strains into the Soviet system. The results of the new thinking in the Soviet Union's international relations have been almost unambiguously positive, not least for those countries of East-Central Europe which from 1989 were given the autonomy to develop along lines they themselves were free to determine. At home, however, the balance-sheet appeared much less impressive to millions of Soviet citizens when so much that was familiar – and at least to that extent reassuring – had been cast aside and the future began to look unsettled and fraught with danger.

Yet, behind the bombast of the Brezhnev era, the reality was that the Soviet Union was falling further behind the rest of the 'civilized world' – to use a term which has acquired popularity in the USSR during the Gorbachev years. The advent of far greater intellectual freedom and the cascade of ideas of remarkable novelty in the Soviet context have, therefore, constituted a necessary prelude to any radical systemic change. The new thinking – in the broadest sense of that term – deserves to be taken seriously and to be welcomed by Western observers for its own sake, for some of the fruits it has already borne – such as the pluralization of Soviet political institutions and the pursuit of a far more enlightened foreign policy – as well as for the further transformation of the Soviet political and economic system which it portends.

Notes

1. M. S. Gorbachev, *Perestroyka i novoe myshlenie dlya nashey strany i dlya vsego mira* (Moscow: Politizdat, 1987).
2. Fedor Burlatsky, *Novoe myshlenie: dialogy i suzhdeniya o tekhnologicheskoy revolyutsii i nashikh reformakh*, 2nd expanded edn (Moscow: Politizdat, 1989).
3. For very useful discussions of the innovative ideas which have been a product of the *glasnost'* of the Gorbachev era in the Soviet Union, see Andrei Melville and Gail W. Lapidus (eds), *The Glasnost Papers: Voices of Reform from Moscow* (Boulder: Westview Press, 1990); Alec Nove, *Glasnost' in Action: Cultural Renaissance in Russia* (London: Unwin Hyman, 1989); and Sylvia Woodby and Alfred B. Evans, Jr., *Restructuring Soviet Ideology: Gorbachev's New Thinking* (Boulder: Westview Press, 1990).
4. S. Alekseev, 'Narastayushchee mnogovlastie', *Literaturnaya gazeta*, 31 October 1990, p. 1.
5. James Farr, 'Understanding Conceptual Change Politically' in Terence Ball, James Farr and Russell L. Hanson (eds), *Political Innovation and Conceptual Change* (Cambridge University Press, 1989), especially pp. 29, 30 and 32.
6. M. Piskotin, 'Nazyvat' veshchi svoimi imenami', *Narodnyy deputat*, no. 11, 1990, pp. 41–50, at p. 46.
7. Ibid.
8. The programme adopted at the Twenty-Eighth Congress of the Communist Party of the Soviet Union in the summer of 1990 was entitled 'Towards a humane and democratic socialism'. (See *Pravda*, 13 July 1990, p. 1.) Gorbachev has more than once used the term, 'totalitarian', to describe the previous Soviet regime, most recently in his opening speech to the April 1991 plenum of the party Central Committee when he declared, in defiance of his hard-line critics, that 'as a result of long-lasting domination by a totalitarian regime our country was threatened with the danger of finding itself on the sidelines of historical progress' (*Pravda*, 24 April 1991, pp. 1–2, at p. 2). A series of books with the general title, *Perestroyka: Glasnost', Demokratiya, Sotsializm*, published by Progress in Moscow, has made a special contribution to the

elaboration of the New Thinking. The first book in the series, edited by Yuriy Afanas'ev and called *Inogo ne dano* (There is no other way), made a particularly great impression when it first appeared in the summer of 1988. It brought together some of the most notable Soviet reformers and broached many previously taboo subjects. Other works in the series include A. N. Zav'yalova (ed.), *Postizhenie* (Moscow: Progress, 1989); Kh. Kobo (ed.), *Osmyslit' kul't Stalina* (Moscow: Progress, 1989); A. G. Vishnevsky, *V chelovecheskom izmerenii* (Moscow: Progress, 1989); M. I. Melkumyan (ed.), *Drama obnovleniya* (Moscow: Progress, 1990); M. P. Vyshinsky, *Pravo i vlast'* (Moscow: Progress, 1990); A. A. Protashchik (ed.), *Cherez ternin* (Moscow: Progress, 1990); A. I. Prokopenko (ed.), *SSSR: Demograficheskiy diagnoz* (Moscow: Progress, 1990); V. E. Kachanov (ed.), *Armiya i obshchestvo* (Moscow: Progress, 1990); M. Ya. Lemeshev (ed.), *Ekologicheskaya al'ternativa* (Moscow: Progress, 1990); N. A. Simoniya (ed.), *SSSR v mirovom soobshchestve: ot starogo myshleniya k novomu* (Moscow: Progress, 1990); and T. A. Notkina, *Pogruzhenie v tryasinu (anatomiya zastoya)* (Moscow: Progress, 1991). In a different series, a work worth special mention is the 1990 yearbook of the Soviet Association of Political Sciences: see D. A. Kerimov (ed.), *Novoe politicheskoe myshlenie i protsess demokratizatsii* (Moscow: Nauka, 1990).

 9. *Sovetskaya Rossiya*, 22 January 1991, p. 2.
10. *Sovetskaya Rossiya*, 6 February 1991, pp. 1–2.
11. *Sovetskaya Rossiya*, 6 February 1991, p. 3.
12. *Pravda*, 12 December 1990, p. 3.
13. See, for example, a small-circulation work compiled in the Bogomolov institute (which until 1990 bore the name, Institute of Economics of the World Socialist System): A. P. Butenko *et al.*, *Problemy ideologicheskogo obnovleniya sotsializma* (Moscow: IEMSS, 1988).
14. Gorbachev's book, *Perestroyka*, cited in note 1, was one of the milestones on the road to new thinking, although Gorbachev's views have continued to develop and change since then. It should not, therefore, be cited – as it sometimes is, perhaps because of its ready accessibility in English translation – as the definitive statement of Gorbachev's political beliefs. More innovative than some of its critics realized at the time, the book does not go nearly so far towards embracing political pluralism and a market economy as Gorbachev was to go in 1989 and 1990.
15. Another important publication from the point of view of development of new thinking in the Soviet Union was an article, 'On the achievement of a qualitatively new Soviet society and the social sciences', by Aleksandr Yakovlev. In its abbreviated and most widely-read version, it was published in *Kommunist*, no. 8, 1987. The full text, which was first given by Yakovlev as a lecture at the Academy of Sciences of the USSR on 17 April 1987, was published in *Vestnik Akademii Nauk SSSR*, no. 6, June 1987, pp. 51–80. Yakovlev's views, like Gorbachev's, have been far from static and though this article was at the time an important stimulus and encouragement to social scientists who wished to break down ideological barriers in their disciplines, by 1990 Yakovlev's thinking had gone further. By then Yakovlev had more explicitly and wholeheartedly

endorsed political pluralism as well as a political agenda still more radically reformist than that of 1987. His contribution to the New Thinking earned him a special place of enmity in the hearts of unreconstructed communists, even though his farewell speech to a party congress (at the Twenty-Eighth Party Congress in July 1990) impressed that predominantly conservative gathering with its sincerity and earned him warmer applause than might have been predicted.

16. *The Third Way* is the title of a book by Ota Šik first published in German in 1972 and in English by Wildwood House, London, in 1976. Šik was a leading economic reformer in Czechoslovakia during the 1960s and one of the makers of the 'Prague Spring' of 1968. The idea of 'The Third Way' was popular at that time both among revisionist Marxists and democratic socialists, but it has lost ground in more recent years, especially in Eastern Europe. After gaining adherents in the Soviet Union in the early years of *perestroika* it began losing some of them as the appeal of existing Western economic and political systems grew stronger in the context of growing economic problems and social unrest in the Soviet Union. The fact that a number of Soviet problems were linked by 1990 to the 'in-between' character of its economy – not the plan *and* market, to which reformers such as Šik had once aspired, but *neither* plan *nor* market – was a further impetus to disillusionment with The Third Way.

2 New Thinking on the Soviet Political System

Archie Brown

In the study of a country which accorded such a central place for so long to an official ideology, Marxism-Leninism, which purported to have all the answers to the major problems of social and political development, the scope and significance of the term, New Political Thinking, becomes a topic of interest. It is touched upon both in the introductory chapter and elsewhere in this volume. Yet *more* important than what that much-used concept connotes in Soviet conventional usage is the fact that there really has been 'new thinking' – the coming to the fore of new ideas – on the Soviet political system as well as on the economy and on the Soviet Union's relations with the rest of the world.

More precisely, there has been thinking which was radically new in terms of the Soviet experience, even if it would be difficult to find within this corpus of writing any ideas which are truly new in the context of the history of political thought. Indeed, it is the reunion of Soviet thinking with other intellectual traditions – mainly Western but also Russian – which marks a qualitative difference between contemporary public discourse in the Soviet Union and that at any previous time of Soviet history. Another novelty is that the political debate is now freer and more wide-ranging than it was even in the 1920s.

THE ORIGINS OF THE NEW THINKING

While the more hospitable political climate of the Gorbachev era has produced qualitative changes in the style and content of political debate in the mass media as well as in specialized books and journals, innovative thought was also developing more gradually throughout the post-Stalin years. The notion, quite popular in the West, that Soviet society in Brezhnev's time could be divided into a tiny minority of dissidents who kept alive independent thought and an overwhelming majority of people who were conformist in thought as well as in behaviour was always a misleading oversimplification. Not only was there a sharp distinction in many cases between public and private discourse, but some conceptual innovation found its way into print, as did esoteric debates, during the period between the mid-1960s and the mid-1980s. The elaboration of more useful categories of political analysis and the covert debates helped to lay the foundation for the new thinking on the Soviet political system which was to become such a striking feature of the Soviet Union in the late 1980s.

Even if we confine our attention to officially published material of the pre-Gorbachev era, we can find advocacy of competitive elections at the local level being made in the 1960s[1] and an extended but esoteric debate on the nature of political power and on the concept of the political system being conducted in the 1970s.[2] Advocates of the development of a discipline of political science strove to break down the absurd dichotomy between the literature on the Communist Party and the literature on 'State and Law', in which the actual role of the Communist Party within the political system was never analyzed. This involved developing the concept of the political system itself, a process in which one of the earliest significant contributions was Fedor Burlatsky's book, *Lenin, The State, Politics*,[3] however tame it may appear by the standards of Soviet writing today.

Burlatsky's extensive writings on the political system (in the abstract, rather than in the concrete terms in which he and many other Soviet authors have written on it in the Gorbachev era) came under conservative attack in Brezhnev's time. Burlatsky was accused, in effect, of being a closet supporter of political pluralism – a serious charge at that time – by his principal opponent, V. S. Shevtsov, a consultant in the Science and Education Department[4] of the Central Committee.[5] Shevtsov's endeavours to portray himself as a defender of Leninism in its purest form and to attack every manifestation of embryonic new political thinking came to an abrupt end, however, in 1982 when he received a lengthy jail sentence for economic crime – having first, and briefly, been moved out of the Central Committee apparatus, so that no stain should attach to higher party officialdom.

At a time of conservatism in the real political world of the Soviet Union, the Brezhnev era saw not insignificant changes in the language of politics. Alongside the familiar terms in the Marxist-Leninist lexicon emerged new ones, including – in addition to 'the political system' (which even became a chapter heading in the 1977 Brezhnev Constitution) – 'political culture', 'political regime', 'political process' and 'political science'.[6]

The two most prominent advocates of the development of a discipline of political science as such were Burlatsky and Georgiy Shakhnazarov who as long ago as 1956 had co-authored an article calling for the development of sociology and who in 1980 argued jointly for 'the development of Marxist-Leninist political science', a project Burlatsky had launched as early as 1965.[7] It is worth noting at this point that, while today – as in the 1960s and 1970s when small groups of overt dissidents called for more far-reaching changes – Burlatsky and Shakhnazarov are not the most radical reformers in the Soviet Union, they have become increasingly influential ones. Shakhnazarov's impact on Gorbachev's thinking and on the shape of political reform is quite direct, for since early 1988 he has been a full-time aide of Gorbachev and his adviser on reform of the political system as well as on what is left of the communist world. Since March 1990 Burlatsky has been editor-in-chief of the weekly newspaper, *Literaturnaya gazeta*, since 1989 an active member of the Supreme Soviet of the USSR, and since 1987 the chairman of an official committee on human rights which has lobbied for reform of the law on emigration and for the abolition of capital punishment.[8]

In the 1970s and first half of the 1980s, a substantial number of Soviet authors discussed Soviet political developments as an esoteric part of their analyses of developments in other countries, whether the Third World[9] or China.[10] Other writers, in the guise of discussing states or bureaucracies in general, made telling points about the Soviet Union in particular. One such political analyst, who was unusually well-informed about Western political science and political thought, was Valeriy Kalensky. (Kalensky, unlike many within-system reformers of the Brezhnev era, did not become a more overt and influential reformer in the Gorbachev years. He applied to leave the Soviet Union in Chernenko's time and emigrated in 1985, soon after Gorbachev had succeeded to the General Secretaryship.) Kalensky, with the Soviet Union firmly in mind but not mentioned explicitly, wrote as early as 1977 about the enormous power concentrated in the hands of *chinovniki* (state bureaucrats), leading 'to the acquisition by that special social stratum of a relative autonomy in relation to the ruling class as a whole, and to its being in certain circumstances even in conflict with it, thrusting upon it selfish interests of its own'.[11] By the 'ruling class' in the Soviet context he had in mind the working class who were accorded that position in official Soviet doctrine, notwithstanding the discrepancy between such a description and reality. Kalensky later published a highly sympathetic study of

James Madison and of his political ideas[12] and his last book to appear in the Soviet Union was a study of the development of civil rights in the United States (which had to be given a more academic and less overtly political title before it could be published) – a sustained, albeit implicit, comparison with the lack of such development in Russia and the Soviet Union.[13]

One stimulus to the new thinking of recent years was the greater contact with and knowledge of the outside world which was already developing in Brezhnev's time and which has accelerated enormously in the Gorbachev era. Another source of the ideas which have become part of the public political discourse on the Soviet political system over the past few years was the earlier activities of dissidents and the development of *samizdat* and *tamizdat*; these were of real significance for a sizeable minority of Soviet intellectuals. But new thinking which owed something to foreign stimulus, something to older traditions of Russian thought and a little to the clandestine writing of dissidents began to take shape in the pages even of Soviet books, journals and newspapers, although the wheat had to be separated from a great deal of chaff. Only a small proportion of the Western political scientists who studied the Soviet Union were adequately aware of the great diversity of view (of which only a few examples have been given here) which lay behind the superficially monolithic façade of publications which had passed through the hands of the state censorship.

NEW THINKING IN THE GORBACHEV ERA

The growth of serious political argument in private in the Soviet Union between 1953 and 1985 and the development of esoteric communication in print during the Brezhnev years – when the social sciences had such dismal, conservative overseers as Mikhail Suslov in the party leadership and Petr Fedoseev in the Academy of Sciences – were by no means as inconsequential occurrences as their relative neglect in the Western literature might suggest. They are major reasons why, with the advent of *glasnost'*, there was a substantial number of Soviet intellectuals ready to publish well-argued political analyses and to extend the frontiers of Soviet political thought. It is not merely in the last six years that they have begun to think about the issues, although equally it is not only – albeit partly – a matter of being able to say plainly in print what they could previously say only behind closed doors or publish in a convoluted form. It is also the case that the ideas of Soviet reformers themselves have become more radical in the course of overt debate and in response to the failures as well as the successes of *perestroika*.

As the examples in the preceding section indicate, it was possible for manuscripts containing independent thought on political subjects to reach the discerning Soviet reader even when they had been through the hands of Glavlit. Yet, in so far as books, newspapers and journals remained under party control and the independence of editors was far less than the bolder among them were to create for themselves by the end of the 1980s – in what was, of course, an altogether more propitious political climate – the distinction between 'official' publications and 'unofficial' self publications could be sustained, notwithstanding the fact that the publication of an article in an 'official' journal did not mean that it necessarily reflected the views of officialdom.

In the Soviet Union today there are two important differences from the Brezhnev era with respect to publications on the political system. In the first place, a number of 'official' newspapers and journals have published materials which go well beyond what is approved by the Central Committee of the Soviet Communist Party. That has been true at various times of, for example, *Argumenty i fakty, Vek XX i mir, Novyy mir, Moscow News* and *Ogonek*. Secondly, as already noted in the previous chapter, independent newspapers are now openly on sale in the Soviet Union – not only in the Baltic republics or the Caucasus but on the streets of Moscow. New political parties have their own newspapers – such as the Social Democrats' *Novaya zhizn'* – even if they are for the most part produced on a shoestring. It would be difficult to think of views from any part of the political spectrum – from monarchist to anarchist – which cannot be published in some form or other, as previously heterodox ideas have begun to acquire an organizational base. (Already in the summer of 1990 an issue of *Moscow News* could discuss eleven political parties or quasi-parties which had been formed since 1988 in addition to the nationalist parties to be found in most republics.[14] Many more parties have been established since then.)

In discussing the extent of the recent changes, I pay particular attention to examples of new thinking on the political system which have appeared in Soviet books, major journals and official newspapers – rather than in the new and more radical press – and note how far such thinking has penetrated the speeches of Gorbachev (in some cases emanating in the first instance from them) and official Communist Party documents. If important change has taken place even there, it indicates the extent of the impact of new ideas in eroding the discredited ideology of Marxism-Leninism.

The role in promoting new thinking on the political system played by the Inter-Regional Group of reformist deputies within the Congress of People's Deputies of the USSR is worth special mention. Although a minority within that legislature, members of the group became opinion leaders within the country where their popularity, as measured by surveys of public opinion, was soon greater than their share of support in the Congress of People's Deputies would suggest. The speed of change in political consciousness within Soviet society has been such that no body elected in the first half of 1989 – in elections, moreover, that retained substantial elements of 'guided democracy' – could be representative of public opinion even a year later. Thus, the legislatures elected in the fifteen Union republics in 1990 became repositories of more radical reformist sentiment and of proposals for changing the Soviet political system than the all-Union Congress and Supreme Soviet. A particularly important case in point has been the legislature of the Russian republic (RSFSR), in addition to which six of the new assemblies – those of Lithuania, Latvia, Estonia, Georgia, Armenia and Moldova (formerly Moldavia) – have gone even further and opted for the break-up of the Soviet Union and the pursuit of independent statehood.

So many important new concepts have come to occupy a central place in Soviet political discourse over the past few years that some will be mentioned only in passing – the concepts of civil society (*grazhdanskoe obshchestvo*), of democratic socialism (which prior to the Gorbachev era was castigated as an archetypically revisionist notion), and of the state based on the rule of law (*pravovoe gosudarstvo*), to name just a few which are now seen as laudable goals not only by radicals but by Gorbachev and even those in the middle of the Soviet political spectrum. On the other side of the coin, there is the increasing application to the unreformed Soviet system of such terms (regarded as 'bourgeois falsifications' a few short years ago) as 'authoritarian' or even 'totalitarian'[15] or – in the words of the programme adopted by the Twenty-Eighth Congress of the Communist Party – 'the statisation (*ogosudarstvlenie*) of all aspects of social life, the dictatorship of the party-state bosses in the name of the proletariat'.[16]

The three elements in the new thinking on the Soviet political

system to which somewhat more detailed attention will be devoted
are: 1. the debate over the 'leading role' of the Communist
Party; 2. the growth of support for 'separation of powers' and
'checks and balances'; and 3. the introduction and development of
the idea of pluralism in Soviet political discourse.

THE LEADING ROLE OF THE PARTY

For years the idea of the 'leading role' of the Communist Party was
one of the key ideological pillars of the Soviet political system. It is
remarkable that this became a subject of serious argument in the
Gorbachev era and that it has led to the redefinition of the concept by
the party leadership, to its radical rejection by many others, and to its
partial erosion in political practice. The Congress of People's Deputies of the USSR in 1989 was the scene of the first public debate on
the need to remove the guaranteed leading role of the Party from
Article 6 of the Constitution. The demands of Andrey Sakharov and
others were resisted at the time by Gorbachev who clearly felt a
political need to bring this forward in due course as an initiative of his
own and of the Communist Party. Since the issue was raised in the
Soviet legislature by Sakharov and a group of fellow-radicals, it is
doubtful whether even an instant capitulation by Gorbachev would
have commanded majority support at that time within the Congress
of People's Deputies, given both the composition and disposition of
that body. It was in March 1990, on the recommendation of Gorbachev himself (who first had to cajole the Central Committee into
approving the change), that the guaranteed leading role of the Communist Party was removed from the Soviet Constitution. This in
itself, of course, did not settle the issue of the Party's role in the
political system. After all, it was only from the time of the fourth
(1977) Constitution that the leading role of the Communist Party had
been enshrined in the country's fundamental law, whereas the Party's
monopoly of power had existed for decades.

The Inter-Regional Group of Deputies produced an important
document at the time of the Second Congress of People's Deputies
(signed by ninety-four deputies) in late 1989 entitled 'On Perestroika
Today and in the Foreseeable Future'.[17] It called for the removal of
the 'infamous sixth article' from the Constitution and argued that if
the Communist Party was to play a leading role in the future it should
be as a result of having won free elections in fair competition with

other parties.[18] The legitimizing of the principle of a multi-party system had begun in 1988. Boris Kurashvili of the Institute of State and Law in Moscow was one of the first to espouse the idea in print while Viktor Sheynis of IMEMO had prior to the changes in Eastern Europe of 1989 called for the Communist Party to cease to be 'a party-state', a phenomenon he associated with African countries, and to become a 'normal political party, with normal European functions' which would mean that it would then not be the only one in the political arena.[19]

In their document already cited, the Inter-Regional Group of Deputies not only welcomed in 1989 the principle of a competitive party system but looked forward to a split in the ranks of the Communist Party, arguing that it was both unavoidable and desirable that the CPSU should split and that it should become 'two or three mass parties in Russia, not to speak about the separation of some republican parties'.[20] They also welcomed the principle of political opposition, observing: 'Without opposition normal political existence is not possible'.[21] The collapse of communism throughout most of Eastern Europe was, of course, a powerful additional stimulus to acceptance of the principle of a multi-party system.

For many in the Communist Party the principle of a multi-party system and the idea of legitimized opposition have been difficult pills to swallow, but Gorbachev in 1990 accepted the former and by implication the latter, even though the Twenty-Eighth Party Congress was unpersuaded. It is of interest that one of the changes made to the draft programmatic statement of the Congress published on 27 June 1990 in the final version published on 15 July was removal of the word, *'mnogopartiynost'* from the section headed 'Civil Society and the Law-Governed State'. In the draft one of the goals the Communist Party was said to be striving for was 'a multi-party system (*mnogopartiynost'*) and the free competition of socio-political organizations within a constitutional framework'.[22] In the final version they were advocating simply 'the free competition of socio-political organizations within a constitutional framework'.[23]

Gorbachev has, however, accepted the developing reality as well as the principle of a competitive party system. In addition, having to a considerable extent turned the tables on his conservative opponents at the Twenty-Eighth Congress of the PSU following their success at the Founding Congress of the Communist Party of the RSFSR in June 1990, Gorbachev made a first attempt to establish a new 'centre-left' coalition designed to include some of those who had already left the

Communist Party. The team of economists, headed by Stanislav Shatalin, which was set up jointly by Gorbachev and Yel'tsin, produced a document which was certainly an example of new thinking in its total break with past Soviet ideology and its pursuit of speedy privatization and marketization.

Officially called 'The Transition to the Market: Concept and Programme',[24] and popularly known as the 'Five Hundred Days Plan', it was partially abandoned by Gorbachev (in favour of a compromise document drawn up by Abel Aganbegyan) under intense pressure from the Council of Ministers, including its Chairman at that time, Nikolay Ryzhkov, the army and the KGB. Yet Gorbachev had already advocated earlier in 1990 the idea of a 'broad coalition' to overcome the crisis and to implement 'profound reforms' – proclaimed in the Congress resolution on the political report of the Central Committee – emphasizing the need to show in practice that this was not merely a tactical move but a serious proposal in the interests of the country and the people.[25]

After a series of concessions during the winter of 1990–1 to opponents of both the new thinking and the new practice – under a degree of duress, the intensity of which is still a matter of debate – Gorbachev in April 1991 moved to mend fences with the radicals and liberals whom he had alienated and, in particular, to end the 'war of laws' which had since the autumn of 1990 characterized relations between the all-Union legislature and the legislatures of a number of Union republics, including the Russian republic. On 23 April he came to a potentially important agreement with the leaders of nine of the Soviet republics, including the non-party and hitherto oppositional-minded Yel'tsin.[26] Together with the shift of power from party institutions to the Presidency which Gorbachev had engineered in early 1990, this represented a further redefinition and dilution of the 'leading role' of the Party.[27]

'CHECKS AND BALANCES' AND 'SEPARATION OF POWERS'

In pre-*perestroika* writing on political systems the concepts of separation of powers and of checks and balances were generally treated as no more than smokescreens behind which the bourgeoisie exercised unfettered power in Western countries. One of the exceptions to that general rule was Kalensky who, in his book on James Madison published in 1981 (to which reference has already been made), devoted a lengthy and judicious chapter to 'The concept of "checks and balances" (*sderzhek i protivovesov*) and the problem of separation of powers'.[28]

It was only in 1987, however, that the idea of checks and balances was advocated in print in the Soviet Union as an institutional arrangement of explicit relevance to Soviet needs. A meeting of the Soviet Association of Political Sciences – at which Georgiy Shakhnazarov presided – discussed the notion in February of that year and a report of the meeting published in *Sovetskoe gosudarstvo i pravo* in July drew attention to the call which had been made for the development of 'a socialist theory of checks and balances' and for the study of both Western practice and the Western theoretical literature on the subject. This was linked to the need to prevent in the Soviet Union the excessive concentration of power in the hands of any one institution or individual.[29]

It was in late 1988 that Gorbachev gave his first endorsement of the idea of checks and balances in the context of recommending the setting-up of the Committee for Supervision of the Constitution (which has indeed now been established, although thus far its institutional impact has not been profound). He referred to 'our own socialist system of "checks and balances" taking shape in this country, designed to protect society against any violation of socialist legality at the highest state level'.[30] Since Shakhnazarov is one of Gorbachev's principal speech-writers, it is reasonable to deduce that he was the author of Gorbachev's reference to 'checks and balances'. Even if these checks and balances were qualified by the adjective, 'socialist', the endorsement of such a principle amounted to another important example of new thinking on the political system at the highest official level. The evident role of Shakhnazarov in no way detracted from the significance of the party General Secretary and Soviet head of state embracing the idea of checks and balances, for Gorbachev is not the kind of leader who has permitted words to be put into his mouth before he was ready to use them.

The principle of separation of powers has also made great strides in terms of high-level endorsement within the Soviet system. In the programmatic statement accepted by the Twenty-Eighth Congress of the Soviet Communist Party in July 1990 a separate sub-section was devoted to it. The programme declared: 'The separation of powers into the legislative, executive, and judicial will create guarantees against the usurpation of unlimited authority and abuse of power and will allow spheres of competence and accountability to be clearly delineated'.[31]

Among the particular points emphasized under the heading of separation of powers in that Communist Party policy document were the importance of annual reports of executive and administrative bodies to soviets; the need for independence of the courts and the procuracy; and the necessity of creating, in effect, a new-style civil service with entry based (presumably) on competitive examination. (The precise wording of the last recommendation is 'the creation of a dynamic, modern state apparatus, formed on a competitive basis, subordinate to representative organs and to the public within the framework of the law'.)[32]

In view of the past performance of the Soviet Communist Party, and the continuing interest of its apparatus in holding on to as many levers of control as possible, a more convincing endorsement of the principle of separation of powers may be that contained in the draft Constitution of the Russian republic drawn up by a working group whose secretary was the young social democrat, Oleg Rumyantsev.[33] Although other variants of a Constitution for the RSFSR were being discussed and debated throughout the winter of 1990–1, the draft of Rumyantsev's group was the one most favoured by the Chairman of the Supreme Soviet of the Russian republic, Boris Yel'tsin. In the draft, Article 1.5 is headed 'The Separation of Powers' and it begins by stating clearly that 'the Russian state is based on the principle of separation . . . of powers – legislative, executive and judicial'. The draft article goes on to say that executive power is vested in the head of state, the President (*Prezident*) of the Russian republic; legislative power belongs to the Parliament (*Parlament*), for which the alternative name of State Duma (*Gosudarstvennaya Duma*) is given; and 'the judicial power is exercised only by the courts'.[34] Both the language used (the terminology is a mixture of the Western and pre-revolutionary Russian) and the substance of the ideas in this draft Constitution as a whole are such that the document represents a very sharp break with all previous Soviet political doctrine.

In reality, however, the separation of powers and checks and balances that operated in the Soviet political system between the summer of 1990 and the spring of 1991 took a somewhat pathological form. The fact that parliaments at the all-Union (federal) level and at the republican levels had enough power to pass contradictory laws but insufficient authority (in the case of the centre) or power (in the case of the republics) to enforce these laws or to pursue a coherent economic strategy was in danger of discrediting principles which had a great deal to commend them in the light of the extreme concentration and abuse of executive power, and the absence of checks upon it, which had been such major features of Soviet history, above all in Stalin's time. What the system still lacked was a Constitution that commanded respect and provided reasonably clear lines of demarcation of jurisdiction as well as an experienced and independent judiciary which could adjudicate in cases of dispute. It also lacked – at least until April 1991 (and it remains to be seen what the future beyond that will hold) – a necessary spirit of political compromise.

FROM MONISM TO PLURALISM

In many instances the new thinking on the Soviet political system has first been enunciated by intellectuals or by elected deputies and has only subsequently been accepted by Gorbachev, but in the case of one key concept in particular, it was the General Secretary who broke the public taboo on its endorsement. The concept in question is 'pluralism' and it serves as a good example of Gorbachev's capacity, on the one hand, to give a lead and, on the other, of his willingness to follow enlightened opinion, for his initial endorsement of pluralism was a heavily qualified one and it was only in 1990 that he gave his personal imprimatur to the concept of 'political pluralism' as distinct from 'socialist pluralism' or a 'pluralism of opinion'.[35]

Stress on the monist character of the Soviet state and on the 'monolithic unity of party and people' were constant themes of Soviet political writing over many years. Attacks on the notion of pluralism became particularly frequent after the concept had been adopted by the 'Prague Spring' reformers of 1968 and was subsequently taken up by 'Eurocommunists' in the 1970s. When Gorbachev put more radical political reform on the agenda in 1987 he and his advisers became increasingly aware that to continue to endorse attacks on pluralism was to play into the hands of their conservative communist opponents. Yet such were the taboos on speaking positively about pluralism that as recently as the early years of *perestroika* no one with less authority than the General Secretary of the Communist Party could get away with breaking them.

It was at a meeting with Soviet writers in July 1987 that Gorbachev first used the term, 'socialist pluralism', in the quite limited sense of opening up the pages of Soviet newspapers to a wider range of

writers. He gradually extended the meaning, so that 'socialist pluralism' became an ideological justification not only for diversity of view
('pluralism of opinion') within the society but for open political
debate and for the creation of pressure groups. Others quickly
followed Gorbachev in the use of the term 'pluralism', and soon
began to extend its scope and significance. The adjective 'socialist',
was often dropped and more and more contributors to the discussion
advocated 'political pluralism' – among them Anatoli Adamishin (at
that time Deputy Minister of Foreign Affairs).[36]

It was in February 1990 that Gorbachev himself began to use the
expression, 'political pluralism', accepting it in principle at the same
time as he accepted the principle of a multi-party system.[37] The
connection was a logical one, for a fully-fledged political pluralism
implies the right of creation of political parties as well as of organized
independent groups. It is a concept, however, which is still resented
by many within the party apparatus who see it, rightly, as undermin-
ing their former ideological hegemony and actual political power.

It goes without saying, therefore, that acceptance of the principle
of political pluralism – in so far as it is accepted – represents a
momentous change. The same is true of endorsement of the principle
of ideological pluralism. The implications of the latter doctrinal shift
have been brought out by Andrei Melville, formerly a department
head at the Institute of the USA and Canada in Moscow and today
one of the Soviet Union's leading independent political analysts, who
has observed:

> The recognition not only of the fact but of the *validity of ideologi-
> cal pluralism* is a logical consequence of the recognition of the
> freedom of social choice. The equal right of every ideology to exist
> is incompatible with claims to the possession of 'absolute truth',
> with our traditional postulate that only one ideology is 'genuinely
> scientific' and expresses the interests of 'the absolute majority of
> the human race' or of 'all progressive forces', while another
> ideology is 'unscientific' and serves 'reactionary interests'.[38]

The extent of the change in the attitude to pluralism in the Soviet
Union can be illustrated by a comparison of the entry on pluralism in
the 1987 edition of the *Kratkiy politicheskiy slovar'* (Short Political
Dictionary)[39] and the entry on 'political pluralism' in the 'Political
Vocabulary' section of the Communist Party journal, *Dialog*, in the
summer of 1990.[40] The former pours cold water over the claims of

'bourgeois sociology' that pluralism represents a 'pure' or 'higher' form of democracy and notes equally disparagingly the use of the concept by Eurocommunists who mistakenly believed that there could be a variety of 'models' of socialism and failed to recognize 'the international character of Marxism-Leninism and the general laws of development of socialist revolution and the construction of socialism'.[41]

The 1990 Soviet entry, in contrast, noted that the term, 'pluralism', had been more and more often used to delineate important aspects of *perestroika* and, above all, 'the deep and all-round democratization of the society and fundamental reorganization of the political system'. It is portrayed as contrasting sharply with 'the Stalinist-Brezhnevite administrative-command system of government' and with any kind of political monopolism. 'Political pluralism' is seen as 'an effective instrument for the establishment of full democracy' and is linked to the legitimization of political opposition.[42]

SOME CONCLUSIONS

Hypotheses about the serious differences of political opinion lying behind pre-1985 Soviet debate on issues of political language and doctrine – ignored by many Western observers at the time and dismissed by others as of no consequence – have been substantially confirmed by the development of political debate in the Gorbachev era. Soviet scholars who, in the twenty years preceding *perestroika*, helped to change the vocabulary of politics, have emerged openly as radical reformers wishing to change the substance of the Soviet political system.

A comparison of Soviet public discourse at the beginning of 1985 and in 1990 shows a qualitative change in the scope and nature of political argument. Its main features are: 1. the transition from esoteric to open debate; 2. the progression from system-adaptive to system-transformative proposals for change; and 3. the ending of the mutual isolation of 'within-system' reformers, on the one hand, and dissidents, on the other. There has been increasing interaction between those who belonged to these two categories as previously 'within-system' reformers have come to advocate views which would make the Soviet system different in kind and as former dissidents have been allowed to play a major part in the political process. Among the more striking instances of the latter phenomenon were the late Andrey Sakharov's election to the Congress of People's Deputies – from the Academy of Sciences – and his appointment to the Constitutional Commission (whose task is to produce a new Constitution for the USSR) and Roy Medvedev's election to the Supreme Soviet as well as to the Congress of People's Deputies in 1989 and, one year after being readmitted to party membership, his election to the Central Committee of the Communist Party in July 1990.

New thinking on the Soviet political system has now proceeded apace along with rapidly changing political practice. But it is important to note that the new thinking preceded the new practice. Some of the groundwork for this was laid in difficult conditions long before Gorbachev succeeded Chernenko as party leader, but over the past six years (and especially between 1987 and 1990) there has been what amounts to a conceptual revolution as well as a radical reform of the political system. Concepts which had either been marginalized by Soviet Marxism-Leninism or which had no place at all within that tradition have been brought into the forefront of political discourse. The fierce resistance which many of those with a vested interest in the unreformed political system are continuing to put up to conceptual innovation (which they identify as 'ideological subversion') remains sufficient testimony to the practical importance of the new thinking on the political system.

Notes

1. See Ronald J. Hill, *Soviet Politics, Political Science and Reform* (Oxford: Martin Robertson, 1980), pp. 23–40.
2. For a discussion of this esoteric debate, see Archie Brown, 'Political Power and the Soviet State: Western and Soviet Perspectives', in Neil Harding (ed.), *The State in Socialist Society* (London: Macmillan, 1984), pp. 53–101.
3. Fedor Burlatsky, *Lenin, Gosudarstvo, Politika* (Moscow: Nauka, 1970).
4. That department of the Central Committee was abolished in the autumn of 1988.
5. See, for example, V. S. Shevtsov, *Gosudarstvennyy suverenitet* (Moscow: Nauka, 1979).
6. I have discussed these in 'Political Power and the Soviet State' in Harding (ed.), *The State in Socialist Society* (see note 2), pp. 51–103; 'Soviet Political Culture through Soviet Eyes' in Archie Brown (ed.), *Political Culture and Communist Studies* (London: Macmillan, 1984),

pp. 100–14; and 'Political Science in the USSR' in *International Political Science Review*, vol. 7 (1986), no. 4, pp. 443–81.

7. F. M. Burlatsky and G. Kh. Shakhnazarov, 'Obshchestvennye nauki i zhizn'', *Literaturnaya gazeta*, 24 March 1956, pp. 3–4; F. M. Burlatsky, 'Politika i nauka', *Pravda*, 10 January 1965, p. 4; and G. Kh. Shakhnazarov and F. M. Burlatsky, 'O razvitii marksistsko-leninskoy politicheskoy nauki', *Voprosy filosofii*, no. 12, December 1980, pp. 10–22.

8. For brief biographies of Burlatsky and Shakhnazarov, see Archie Brown (ed.), *The Soviet Union: A Biographical Dictionary* (London: Weidenfeld and Nicolson, 1990 and New York: Macmillan, 1991), pp. 61–2 and 331–2.

9. See, for example, L. A. Reysner and N. A. Simoniya (eds), *Evolyutsiya vostochnykh obshchestv: sintez traditsionnogo i sovremennogo* (Moscow: Nauka, 1984).

10. Gilbert Rozman, *A Mirror for Socialism: Soviet Criticisms of China* (Princeton University Press, N.J., 1985).

11. V. G. Kalensky, *Gosudarstvo kak ob'ekt sotsiologicheskogo analiza* (Moscow: Yuridicheskaya literatura, 1977), p. 122. See also Kalensky's *Politicheskaya nauka v SShA: kritika burzhuaznykh kontseptsii vlasti* (Moscow: Yuridicheskaya literatura, 1969).

12. V. G. Kalensky, *Medison* (Madison) (Moscow: Yuridicheskaya literatura, 1981).

13. V. G. Kalensky, *Bill' o pravakh v konstitutsionnoy istorii SShA* (Moscow: Nauka, 1983).

14. *Moscow News*, no. 28, 22–9 July 1990, pp. 8–9.

15. As noted in Chapter 1, even Gorbachev has applied these pejorative terms to the system he inherited and in which he worked his way up to the highest rungs of the political ladder. Earlier and more elaborate use of these concepts to analyze the Soviet system were made by intellectual critics in the series of innovative books launched by *Inogo ne dano* and published by Progress (as noted in Chapter 1, note 8). An interesting article by Andranik Migranyan places the Soviet Union in a comparative-historical discussion of the transition from 'totalitarian-authoritarian regimes to democracy'. See A. Migranyan, 'Reforma politicheskoy sistemy: kuda ona vedet?', in V. I. Mukomel' (ed.), *SSSR: demograficheskiy diagnoz* (Moscow: Progress, 1990). See also L. Ya. Gozman and A. M. Etkind, 'Lyudi i vlast': ot totalitarizma k demokratii', in A. G. Vishnevsky (ed.), *V chelovecheskom izmerenii* (Moscow: Progress, 1989).

16. *Pravda*, 15 July 1990, p. 1.

17. 'O perestroyke segodnya i v obozrimom budushchem: zayavlenie narodnykh deputatov SSSR-chlenov mezhregional'noy gruppy' in *Vek XX i mir*, no. 2, 1990, pp. 42–8.

18. Ibid., pp. 44–5.

19. V. L. Sheynis, in '"Kruglyy stol": Plyuralizm v sotsialisticheskom obshchestve: puti utverzhdeniya v usloviyakh perestroyke', *Vestnik Moskovskogo universiteta: Seriya 12: Teoriya nauchnogo kommunizma*, no. 4, July–August 1989, pp. 3–72, at p. 39.

20. *Vek XX i mir*, no. 2, 1990, at p. 45.

21. Ibid.
22. *Pravda*, 27 June 1990, p. 2.
23. *Pravda*, 15 July 1990, p. 3.
24. *Perekhod k rynku. Kontseptsiya i programma* (Moscow: Arkhangel's-koe, August 1990).
25. *Pravda*, 14 July 1990, p. 1.
26. *Pravda*, 24 April 1991, p. 1.
27. In practice the extent to which the Communist Party exercised its leading role varied enormously from one part of the country to another by the spring of 1991. In the Baltic republics and Georgia, for instance, it had been voted out of office and had in fact ceased to rule.
28. Kalensky, *Medison* (Madison) (Moscow: Yuridicheskaya literatura, 1981), pp. 65–100.
29. S. E. Deytsev and I. G. Shablinsky, 'Rol' politicheskikh institutov v uskorenii sotsial'no-ekonomicheskogo razvitiya', in *Sovetskoe gosudarstvo i pravo*, no. 7, July 1987, p. 120.
30. *Pravda*, 30 November 1988, p. 2.
31. *Pravda*, 15 July 1990, p. 3.
32. Ibid.
33. *Konstitutsiya (osnovnoy zakon) rossiyskoy federatsii: Proekt rabochey gruppy i gruppy ekspertov* (Moscow: Dom Sovetov RSFSR, 19 October 1990).
34. Ibid., pp. 5–6.
35. *Pravda*, 6 February 1990, pp. 1–2, at p. 1.
36. Anatoli Adamishin, 'Humanity's Common Destiny', in *International Affairs* (Moscow), no. 2, February 1989, p. 11.
37. *Pravda*, 6 February 1990, pp. 1–2, at p. 1.
38. Andrei Melville, 'What's "New" about the "New Political Thinking"?', Paper prepared for the Cato Institute conference on 'Transition to Freedom: The New Soviet Challenge' in Moscow, September 10–14 1990, p. 26.
39. *Kratkiy politicheskiy slovar'* (Moscow: Politizdat, 1987), p. 342–3.
40. *Dialog*, no. 7, 1990, p. 59.
41. *Kratkiy politicheskiy slovar'* (Moscow: Politizdat, 1987), p. 342–3.
42. *Dialog*, no. 7, 1990, p. 59.

3 New Thinking on the Soviet Economy

Alec Nove

About a quarter of a century has gone by since Wassili Leontief wrote 'The fall and rise of Soviet economics'. And indeed at that time there had already been a marked recovery from the miserable state into which the discipline had been plunged in Stalin's time. One can only note with regret and a kind of nostalgia the high quality of the profession in the 1920s: Aleksandr Chayanov (peasant agriculture and cooperation), Nikolay Kondrat'ev (long and short cycles, growth theory), Vladimir Bazarov (theories of value and of socialist industrialization), L. Yurovsky and S. Fal'kner (money and finance), Vladimir Groman and Pavel Popov (balances of the national economy) were men of great distinction. All were destroyed.

After Stalin died it took a few years for members of the profession to get off their knees. In 1955 V. Dyachenko took his colleagues to task for timid 'quotationism'. He added, 'The elaboration of key problems of the national economy is most backward. For years not a single solid theoretical work in this field has been published'.[1] It is hard to blame the individuals concerned. They wished to go on living. Interestingly, in his last work Stalin vigorously attacked one Yaroshenko, who had wished to define economics as the study of the organization of production and distribution. Some in the West speculated – since no one had heard of Yaroshenko – that Stalin had invented a straw-man. So it was a surprise for me, when I attended a discussion in Moscow in November 1989, to see none other than Yaroshenko himself (now aged ninety) tell the audience that he had survived, and was still defending his viewpoint!

Much that was positive happened in the following ten years. The 'legitimation' of mathematical economics, of input–output techniques, of cybernetics, the foundation of the Economico-Mathematical Institute, the ideas of Leonid Kantorovich and Viktor Novozhilov, arguments with the remaining dogmatists about the meaning and relevance of the Marxist labour-theory of value, the publicity given to the ideas of Liberman; these were signs of real intellectual progress. Mention must also be made of the role of Vasiliy Nemchinov, who gave influential support to the spread of new ideas, and the rediscovery of old ones. Such men as Albert Vainshtein, released and rehabilitated, also made significant contributions. A younger generation arose – for example, Nikolay Petrakov and Stanislav Shatalin – which tried with some success to modernize theory and to link it with practice (they are playing a leading role in the reform discussion today). They all had to cope with dogmatists' counter-attacks, with accusations of 'marginalism' and of not being faithful to the labour-theory of value. There were plenty of published criticisms of the malfunctioning of this or that sector of the economy, which enabled Western authors of textbooks to fill them with critical quotations. However, as a number of Soviet colleagues have been pointing out recently, proposals could go no further than 'further perfecting' the existing system. The importance of 'commodity–money relations' was formally recognized, but it was not possible to discuss the desirability and possible extent of markets or the role of prices in resource allocation. The principles of centralized planning could not be challenged. An exception was the pamphlet by Gennadiy Lisichkin, *Plan i rynok* (Plan and Market), published in 1965. The author was heavily criticized and left Moscow for a time.

The support given in those years to mathematical economics may well be explicable by the belief that computerization and programming techniques gave promise of an efficient form of centralized planning. Much work was done to develop 'SOFE' (System of Optimal Functioning of the Economy), a very good study of which was published in English in Helsinki by Pekka Sutela.[2] While intellectually stimulating, and on a much higher level than the dogmatists' economics of socialism, SOFE proved a cul-de-sac. It proved impossible to 'marry' it with an actually functioning economy, not least because it proved impossible to define a meaningful 'objective function'.

Orthodox apologists spun out variations on the theme of 'real' or 'mature' or developed socialism. When, in 1983, scholars in Novosibirsk (notably Tat'yana Zaslavskaya) began to dig deeper, to relate the economic system to social reality and to raise the question of its conformity to the organizational and social-psychological needs of a modern industrial economy, publication of their discussion document was refused, and Zaslavskaya and Abel Aganbegyan were reprimanded for allowing it to be leaked. But the fact that this discussion was taking place serves as a reminder that in those years freedom of speech was much greater than was freedom of the press; much that appeared later was already being debated in the years of so-called stagnation.

There were some taboos before the launching of *perestroika*. Marx, Engels and Lenin were beyond criticism. It was difficult to query official statistics, though some criticisms did begin to appear (I used them in my Manchester Statistical Society paper, 'Has Soviet growth ceased?', published in 1983). There could be no critical analysis of the economies of other communist-ruled countries (unless, like China, they had already been relegated to outer darkness). Western Sovietologists were, with hardly an exception, treated as bourgeois falsifiers.

The advent of *glasnost'* did not transform the situation overnight. As also in some other disciplines, changes were needed in personnel, editors, and so on. But clearly the recognition of the need for radical reform opened wide the area of permissible discussion both about the actual state of the economy and on genuinely radical means of remedying observed ills.

The first published article that sounded loud and clear alarm about the looming crisis of the economy was that of Nikolay Shmelev in *Novyy mir*:

> Today we have an economy characterized by shortages, imbalances, in many respects unmanageable, and to be honest, almost unplannable . . . Apathy, indifference, thieving, have become mass phenomena . . . There is no belief in the officially announced objectives and purposes, or in the very possibility of a more rational economic and social organization of life . . . Things should be given their proper names: stupidity is stupidity, incompetence is incompetence, today's Stalinism is today's Stalinism . . .,[3]

and so on for many pages. Others soon followed his example. During the next three to four years there emerged a picture of startling inefficiency, malfunctioning, waste, losses and misallocation; all these could now be directly and openly given a systemic explanation, rather than be attributed to human error or specific instances of inefficiency.

Official statistics could now also be publicly challenged. The most famous example is the article by Khanin and Selyunin, 'Lukavaya tsifra',[4] which suggested that the official growth of national income from 1928 to 1986, a ninety-fold increase, should be scaled down to an increase of between six and seven times, surely the largest downward amendment of growth rates known in world statistical history. Khanin's ideas were published soon after in the Party's own *Kommunist.* Others joined in. In similar vein, Illarionov, in *EKO*,[5] presented data to show that the Soviet Union is an underdeveloped country at a level similar to that of Venezuela, Portugal or Greece. Others noted the very low position of the USSR in respect of infant mortality, comparable to Mauretania and Barbados. Still others poured scorn on the officially published comparisons of US and Soviet national income. Most recently Soviet scholars have openly circulated papers expressing the view that the CIA substantially overestimates both Soviet growth and the relative size of its GNP and personal consumption.[6] This is not the right context in which to discuss statistics. But these recomputations lead to 'ideological' conclusions of considerable significance: if Khanin, Illarionov and others such are anywhere near correct, then the Soviet Union is as far behind the United States (or perhaps even further) then was the Russian Empire in 1913. This calls for a long, hard, critical look at Soviet economic history, indeed at the entire post-revolutionary experience, and, as we shall see, at the ideological basis of the revolution itself. Thus, to cite just one example, we have S. Dzarasov writing:

How shall we see Soviet experience? Let us not avoid the question by laughable comparisons of our growth with the prerevolutionary period. Other countries did not stand still either . . . The experience of the Soviet Union, despite certain achievements, in the last historical analysis has turned out to be negative. The vast efforts of three human generations, huge sufferings and millions of victims sacrificed on the social altar have not achieved the desired level of progress. The USSR could not achieve this within the framework of the old conception of socialism. Let us look truth in the face. In the eighth decade of its history, our country is still, as in years past, well behind the advanced countries in the basic indicators: technology, the qualifications of the workforce, labour productivity, wages, the quantity and quality of goods and services, social security, human rights.[7]

From which necessarily follows a set of recommendations for very radical, indeed revolutionary change.

There also follows the need for a cool, hard look at Marxism-Leninism itself as well as an attempt (which will not be discussed in detail here) to interpret the nature of Soviet society in and after its Stalinist period. The *nomenklatura*, its privileges, its role as a sort of collective ruling class, may all be freely discussed and debated.[8]

Even the comparatively conservative A. Sergeev could raise the question:

> It is known that Marx and Engels held that socialism and com-
> modity production were not only contradictory but incompatible.
> Lenin took the same view. Even today no one has the theoretical
> effrontery to assert that Lenin was the creator of the theory of
> commodity production under socialism. Was the theory of Marx,
> Engels and Lenin about socialism then wrong. . .?[9]

Gavriil Popov, now also very active in politics, became editor of *Voprosy ekonomiki*, in July 1988. He at once brought with him a new wind. Here is an extract from his first editorial:

> The years of stagnation had serious effects on theory. Scholastics,
> fruitless cleverness, were combined with shameless apologetics for
> any measures taken by the leadership, praising them as if grandiose
> theoretical achievements . . . There was no decisive breakthrough
> in the elaboration of a contemporary model of socialism. Yet after
> Lenin, not to speak of Marx and Engels, there were huge changes
> in the world.

A debate followed on what should be in a new economics textbook. Was Lenin's theory of imperialism wrong? Rakitsy declared that 'we do not live under socialism, but in a barrack-like deformation of socialism'. Popov himself harshly criticized Engel's 'Anti-Duehring'. In fact several of the economists have argued that Duehring was right as against Engels.[10]

During 1989 and even more in 1990 criticism of Marxism-Leninism became ever sharper. It spread even to the Party's own *Kommunist*. In a remarkable article, I. Pantin and E. Plimak had much to say about contradictions in the thought of Marx and Engels; about so-called bourgeois democracy, about the possibilities of planning without a market, about the peasantry. Did they not recommend 'the expropriation of land ownership', apparently including smallhold-ings, compulsory labour in labour armies in town and 'especially' in the countryside? 'As we have seen, Marx and Engels not seldom committed errors, sometimes on matters of principle'.[11]

Lenin too has come under increasing criticism. With the publication of the *Gulag Archipelago*, Vassili Grossman's *Vsyo techyot* and Vladimir Soloukhin's *Chitaya Lenina*, there seems little more that could be printed to his detriment. Less and less does one see the slogan 'back to Lenin'. His own economic *naïveté*, for example his use of the German war-economy model, or the example of the post office, can be freely pointed to. A recent example is V. Yevstigneev in *Voprosy ekonomiki*. After a whole series of critical remarks and telling quotations, it is roundly asserted that

> Socialism, according to Lenin, is a total state monopoly, emerging out of a state-capitalist monopoly, organizing production in a military manner on the basis of 'a single factory', implying a transition to centralized economic control, especially over the workforce. The country is seen as a 'single factory' with commodity exchange excluded (since how can one have commodity exchange between brigades and workshops), with the inevitable domination of non-economic 'disciplinary' obligation to work, governed by a trinity, joined together in a supermonopoly, monopolizing production, employment, and political power and ideology.12

Furthermore, in *Nauka i zhizn'* the prolific Gavriil Popov refers at length to the party programme of 1919, adopted under Lenin's guidance, stressing how closely Stalin stuck to its provisions through all his political life.[13] Earlier in the same journal Popov had coined the phrase 'administrative system' to describe Stalinist centralized planning, and had examined its logic and its *modus operandi*. This was an important stage in the ongoing re-examination both of Stalinism and of the purposes which it served.

This finally brings one to the reform process itself, and to the views of the profession about the causes and remedies of the acute crisis in which the partially-reformed system finds itself today, and to the important and linked question *kuda my idyom* – where are we going, what sort of reform model should there be. One deplores also the lack of any adequate theory or strategy of transition, but of course it is vital to know also where one is supposed to be 'transiting' to.

There have been first class analyses by such men as E. Gaidar[14] and K. Kagalovsky,[15] many statements and interviews by such eminent specialists as Leonid Abalkin, Nikolay Petrakov and Stanislav Shatalin. As the last-named said to a Central Committee plenum in February 1990, 'It is not now a question of saving socialism, communism, or any other -ism, it is a question of saving our people, our country'.[16] There is widespread vigorous criticism of the half-measures so far taken; of the soaring budget deficit, excessive money creation, lack of action on prices, the collapse of control over money wages, the confusions of regional economic autonomy and the problems linked with nationalism (with each republic all too ready to prove that it is exploited by others). Vladimir Tikhonov, the Chairman of the All-Union Society of Cooperators, repeatedly accuses the authorities of obstructing the growing cooperative movement, while the slogan 'land to the peasants' has been rendered inoperative by the fact that *kolkhozy* and *sovkhozy* (backed until recently at the centre by Yegor Ligachev) have no wish to part with their land. This is not the place for yet another account of just what has gone wrong and why. But it is necessary to present some of the evidence concerning the changing views of many prominent economists about a 'regulated market', market socialism, capitalism and the Polish model.

It is something of a thankless task to present a series of highly divergent views, which are rapidly evolving in all sorts of directions. One thing which is notable is the ever-greater freedom of expressing virtually all of them.

As also in Poland, Hungary and Czechoslovakia, the failures of the centralized system and of attempts to reform it have led a number of economists and publicists to abandon the very notion of market socialism and to say, with Kornai, 'there is no third way', that their own earlier notions of combining plan and market in some socialist way were 'naïve'. So far this sort of view is still put forward by a small minority in the Soviet Union, but it is a growing minority. Furthermore, it is possible, or even likely, that a number of prominent economists prefer not to say such things openly, or not yet, bearing in mind not only the views of the leadership but the state of public opinion. For it is a fact that private enterprise, private employment ('exploitation'), private and cooperative trading intermediaries, the entire institutions and 'culture' of the market, are not well regarded by a large segment of the population. So, while such men as Bogomolov, Petrakov, Shatalin, Latsis and Gaidar repeatedly and openly attack the existing reform programme as too little, too late, too much regulation, too little market, it is far from clear what sort of 'socialist' model they have in mind; if indeed they have one.

Meanwhile Pinsker and Pyasheva[17] and Pyasheva[18] (published in Riga) go all the way to a position that is a mixture of Hayek, Friedman and Thatcher, quoting Hayek's *The Road to Serfdom* and denouncing the West European welfare state in the crudest Chicago terms. They both seem to see not only Swedes but even the West German social democrats as dangerous lefties who desire to travel the road to serfdom *slowly*. The 'basis' of socialism can be questioned also by such economists as V. Mau, writing on 'the contradictions of socialist doctrines'.[19]

At the other extreme are the neo-slavophile publicists of *Nash sovremennik* and *Literaturnaya Rossiya*, men such as Aleksandr Prokhanov and Mikhail Antonov, whose economic ideology reminds one of Solzhenitsyn and Dostoevsky: they are against Western commercial culture, are deeply suspicious of marketization and of the penetration of foreign capital and they attack the reforming economists. Outside a Moscow conference hall in November 1989 someone held up a poster, asserting that ABALKIN IS LYSENKO TODAY. Their alternative is less than clear. In conversations with two of them I formed the opinion that they believed in some cleaned-up version of centralized socialist planning with minimal market elements.

In contrast, the journal *Voprosy ekonomiki* (no. 4, 1990) published 'the economic programme of the Democratic Union', which advocates extensive denationalization and privatization. It denounces leasing in agriculture as 'preserving and perfecting state-despotic relations and the preservation of an "Asiatic" type of collectivism', preferring private and genuinely cooperative ownership of land. In the same issue one finds the programme of the 'Confederation of Anarcho-Syndicalists'. So the debate spreads widely in the pages of that monthly. The same issue prints articles by the distinguished American Sovietologist, Joseph Berliner; the Hungarian economist, Laszlo Csaba; and the Japanese scholar, S. Tabata (of Hokkaido). Under Popov's editorship it is certainly lively!

There are all kinds of other views, which it would take too much space even to list, let alone summarize. A good example is V. Dadayan on 'Economics of socialism, aims and means', in *Voprosy ekonomiki*.[20] Here he discusses at length the objectives of social justice and efficiency, property relations and the role of the state, with particular stress laid on social justice as a defining characteristic of socialism. In the same issue R. Nureev tackles another controversial subject: 'The Asiatic mode of production and socialism'. After a critical examination of the concept, the author notes some similarities between it and aspects of Soviet reality, such as the mass use of forced labour. The next article in that same issue discusses the 'compatibility of socialism and entrepreneurship'. Meanwhile senior members of the profession show themselves aware not only of the dangerous consequences of today's economic crisis, but also of the lack of any adequate theory of transition. Shatalin and others advocate the creation of a capital market, the recognition of a market for labour and harsh economic discipline, mitigated by social guarantees. They seek the spread at the earliest date of free market prices, but also realize that their introduction in the present circumstances of acute shortage could lead to a social explosion. This explains why a man like Gavriil Popov, undoubtedly a believer in markets, can advocate having recourse to a (temporary) rationing scheme to deal with immediate emergency, as he did soon after becoming Chairman of the Moscow City Soviet in 1990.

So, on the one hand, the freedom with which a wide variety of views find their way into print must be welcomed. But, on the other, this very wide variety, reflecting also a broad spectrum of political differences, cannot be of much help to a leadership which must be increasingly bemused by the fact that *perestroika* seems to have made things so much worse. One is also conscious that (as is the case also in Hungary and Poland) some economists have taken to idealizing the free markets of the West. The *Boston Globe* published a telling cartoon, under the heading 'Eastern Europe'. A citizen is reading 'The ABC of capitalism'. Under the letter B he finds

BONDS, JUNK
BAILOUT, SAVINGS & LOANS
BUY OUTS, LEVERAGED
BANKRUPTCY

Of course there is much of value to be learned from the experience and the institutions of the West; and rather less from formal mathematicized neo-classical theory, which tends to abstract from important aspects of real competitive markets and neglects institutions. There is urgent need for what could be called relevant economics, inspired neither by Marx nor by Walras.

Meanwhile new ideas proliferate, in a free atmosphere of vigorous debate. But we see also gloom and premonitions of imminent collapse. The old ideological bearings have all but withered away. Some now consider 1917 itself as a disaster and Stalinism as 'the tragedy, responsibility and pain of Bolshevism', to cite one of Tsipko's challenging articles.[21] To bring economic and political order out of threatening chaos a legitimate government must act in the name of –

what? To achieve what sort of just society? To define and build a new sort of socialism? Or is 'socialism the longest road from feudalism to capitalism'?

To paraphrase one of the statements by the radical publicist V. Selyunin: 'We led you the wrong way for seventy years, and in the last five years we ruined the economy. So trust us to lead you, through inflation and unemployment, to a happy future'.[22] Not exactly an inspiring electoral programme for the Communist Party to present. There are now other parties, but also a dearth of constructive alternative strategies. Perhaps by the time these lines are printed there will be a government of national salvation. Or the process of disintegration will continue. *Qui vivra, verra.*

Notes

1. *Voprosy ekonomiki*, no. 10, 1955, pp. 3–4.
2. P. Sutela, '*SOFE*' (Helsinki, 1987).
3. 'Avansy i dolgi', *Novyy mir*, no. 6, 1987, p. 142.
4. *Novyy mir*, no. 2, 1987, p. 181.
5. *EKO*, no. 12, 1988.
6. In papers presented to the conference at Arden House, Virginia, held in April 1990.
7. *Voprosy ekonomiki*, no. 2, 1990.
8. A review-article on these debates by V. Vilchek appears in *Novyy mir*, no. 3, 1990.
9. *Voprosy ekonomiki*, no. 7, 1988.
10. *Voprosy ekonomiki*, no. 10, 1988, and V. Kiselev in Y. Afanasyev (ed.), *Inogo ne dano* (Moscow, 1988) pp. 357–8.
11. *Kommunist*, no. 4, 1990, p. 28.
12. *Voprosy ekonomiki*, no. 3, 1990.
13. G. Popov, in *Nauka i zhizn'*, no. 11, 1989.
14. *Kommunist*, no. 2, 1988, no. 2, 1989, no. 2, 1990, and also *Pravda* 24 and 25 July 1990.
15. *Kommunist*, no. 4, 1990, p. 60.
16. *Pravda*, 20 February 1990.
17. *Novyy mir*, no. 11, 1989, p. 184.
18. *Rodnik*, no. 1, 1990.
19. *Izvestiya Akademii nauk – seriya ekonomicheskaya*, no. 3, 1990.
20. *Voprosy ekonomiki*, no. 3, 1990.
21. *Nauka i zhizn'*, no. 2, 1989.
22. *Literaturnaya gazeta*, 2 May 1990.

4 New Thinking and the National Question[1]

Gail W. Lapidus

INTRODUCTION

The accession of Mikhail Gorbachev to the Soviet leadership, and the inauguration of an increasingly far-reaching programme of reforms, decisively transformed the very nature of the 'National Question' in Soviet political life. The Gorbachev era not only brought the issue to the top of the political agenda; it altered the very premises of the discussion. The 'National Question', in the form in which it had been inherited from the past, ceased to exist. Its place was taken by a major political struggle over the nature and future of the Soviet federation itself, in which sharp cleavages extending to the very top of the Soviet leadership became entwined with the broader struggle over reform.

These cleavages were the product of far-reaching conceptual as well as political changes unleashed by *glasnost'* and democratization. They involved a fundamental shift in the underlying assumptions of Soviet nationality policy, a reassessment of the past history and present condition of national relations, important modifications of key policy concepts, and consideration of a whole range of structural and policy measures that would significantly alter the nature of centre–periphery relations. In short, new political realities were accompanied by the emergence of what amounted to 'New Thinking' about nationality policy, and by a growing recognition within an important segment of the Soviet leadership that a *perestroika* of the federal system was a necessary and indeed inseparable component of the larger process of reform.

It is therefore important to recall that the 'National Question' was never initially a part of the reformist agenda. In launching the entire process of reform, the Soviet leadership – and Gorbachev in particular – never anticipated that the economic and political changes they contemplated would ignite the National Question, and they clearly underestimated its explosiveness. Indeed, Gorbachev himself came to power relatively ill-prepared – both by personal temperament and

39

by previous political experience – to deal with the problem, and when it began to force itself to the centre of his attention, he revealed a certain irritation that such intensely emotional, indeed irrational sentiments and preoccupations could divert attention from the larger struggle over reform.

Nor were reform-minded scholars or intellectuals outside the political establishment any better prepared. By contrast with the discussions of economic and political reform which long antedated Gorbachev's accession to power, the national question was largely absent from their agenda as well. The pervasive conviction that modernization would bring with it the erosion of particularistic loyalties and attachments; the tendency to denigrate national sentiment as atavistic and unworthy of progressive intellectuals; and the assumption that a shared commitment to economic and political reform would unify all progressive forces on an all-Union basis, were shared by reformers inside and outside the political establishment alike.

It was the events of 1986–8 which rudely shattered these assumptions and pushed analysts as well as policymakers toward a fundamental re-thinking of the nature of the Soviet multinational system. 'New Thinking' on the National Question was, therefore, an unintended consequence of political forces unleashed by the reform process rather than one of its sources, and the key actors in this drama were not primarily reform-oriented intellectuals in Moscow think-tanks but cultural elites and political activists in the non-Russian republics.

THE NATIONAL QUESTION IN THE BREZHNEV ERA

Some elements of 'New Thinking' about national relations can be traced back to the Brezhnev era, as ethnographers and sociologists conducting empirical research on ethnic processes began to challenge both the dominant role of party ideologists in defining the issues and some of the conventional assumptions and clichés surrounding their discussion. It suffices to recall such well-worn phrases as the 'flowering and rapprochement of nations', and the 'emergence of a new historical community – the Soviet people', to be reminded of the ideological strait-jacket their efforts confronted.

A major and frequently esoteric debate over terminology which erupted in the mid-1960s reflected an effort by a number of scholars to escape the stifling constraints of Stalinist orthodoxy concerning nations and their development.[2] During the 1970s and early 1980s scholars such as Yulian Bromley, Director of the Academy of Sciences' Institute of Ethnography in Moscow, and a number of colleagues, sought to legitimate the role of ethnographers in analyzing contemporary Soviet ethnic processes and to offer a more complex and subtle treatment of ethnic processes than official ideological positions allowed for.[3] Among the promising new directions pointed to by this work was the effort to add a subjective and psychological dimension to Stalin's definition of 'nation' by making self-consciousness one of its core features, and to suggest that national identity was more enduring and less malleable than had previously been assumed.

But the obligatory tone of self-congratulation which permeated scholarly writings, the continuing ideological constraints surrounding the entire discussion of ethnic processes, and the narrow scope of permissible social science research, limited the ability of Soviet scholars to come to a full understanding of the real character of inter-ethnic relations in Soviet society and to prepare either the political leadership or the public for the problems ahead. As Igor Krupnik summed up the situation:

> The stringent ideological choice of ideas and opinions was intended to cut off all attempts at critical analysis and independent prognosis. The closed nature of demographic, sociological, and practically all contemporary statistical data destroyed for the majority of scientists the possibility of independent creative research and a feedback mechanism in the form of wide-ranging debate and discussion that prompts a response from one's colleagues. Finally, the possibility of analyzing the complicated problems of the day just on the level of closed memoranda or government publications either left only narrowly specialized, predominantly historical themes to the 'open press' or demanded publication of fulsome praise.[4]

Parallel to but distinct from these scholarly controversies, a series of policy debates bearing on the nature and future of the Soviet federal system was also under way in the late Brezhnev era. Two opposing tendencies, with conflicting diagnoses, goals, and recommendations, contended for influence over policy: the first advocating greater political and economic integration and the more rapid assimilation of the non-Russian nationalities, and the second urging greater accommodation by the system to the needs and desires of diverse national groups.

The debates ranged, in extremely Aesopian language, over a whole gamut of sensitive issues: the balance to be struck between a unitary and centralized as opposed to a federal and pluralist conception of the Union; the degree to which resource allocation should continue to be aimed at equalization among republics; the desirability of continuing to pursue 'affirmative action' in higher education and employment; the role of Russian language in the non-Russian republics; and whether to pursue an ethnically-differentiated demographic policy.[5] While the Brezhnev leadership refrained from dramatic new initiatives in these areas, the most visible public challenges to the status quo in the late Brezhnev era came from advocates of a more integrationist, coercive, Russo-centric, and assimilationist approach to these questions.

THE INTEGRATIONIST CHALLENGE IN THE POST-BREZHNEV ERA

This approach appeared to gain additional influence with the accession of Andropov to the Soviet leadership. In his keynote address on the sixtieth anniversary of the formation of the USSR in December 1982, Andropov delivered an unusually sophisticated and far from complacent review of the nationality question. Reminding his audience that numerous problems demanded attention and that they could not be attributed solely to 'survivals of the past', he explicitly called for the formulation of a 'well-thought-out, scientifically substantiated nationalities policy'.[6]

Particularly striking was Andropov's explicit use of the term *sliyanie* (merger or fusion) to describe the ultimate goal of Soviet nationality policy, in a passage quoting Lenin himself. The term had been rarely used during Brezhnev's tenure and had not appeared in the Central Committee decree published under Brezhnev six months earlier announcing the forthcoming anniversary celebration. But it had made a striking reappearance in late 1982 in the speeches and writings of Richard Kosolapov, an important party theoretician and editor-in-chief of *Kommunist*. In an article published at the end of 1982, Kosolapov had explicitly quoted Lenin's words that the goal of socialism was not only to bring about the rapprochement (*sblizhenie*) of nations but their fusion (*sliyanie*) as well. 'As clear a statement as this', he had added, 'leaves no room for reinterpretation'.[7] Kosolapov had gone on to criticize the attempts of 'some social scientists' to either ignore Lenin's views on the subject or, worse still, to depict them as a form of Great Russian chauvinism. 'To put it bluntly', he had asserted, 'only a few years ago comrades who insisted on developing the idea of fusion in unadulterated form and comparing it with practice found themselves in a difficult situation with some scholarly organizations and journals. . .'.[8]

Clearly, Andropov's tenure in office was too brief to ascertain with any confidence whether his nationalities policies would in fact have taken the more coercive direction these statements imply. But insofar as the initial Gorbachev coalition essentially inherited Andropov's programme, and pursued it during its first months in power, the evidence suggests that key elements of the integrationist strategy had been adopted by the new leadership as part of its approach to reform.

This programme embraced three broad goals: first, to reassert effective central control over the strategic levers of power which had slipped away under Brezhnev, by curtailing the excessive independence of local political machines and conducting purges of their key personnel; secondly, to arrest the deterioration of economic performance that jeopardized both domestic stability and international power by shifting from an extensive to an intensive pattern of economic development and pressing for economic acceleration and modernization; and thirdly, to revive declining civic morale and restore a sense of social discipline by campaigns targeted at what were perceived as two major and visible sources of social corrosion: corruption and alcoholism.

The 'National Question' did not figure directly in this strategy: it aimed at rationalizing economic and political organization on an all-Union scale, and emphasizing efficiency over equity, in the interest of strengthening both control and performance. But in the multinational and federal context of Soviet politics, this agenda would inevitably impinge differentially on the interests of different national elites. What the Gorbachev leadership failed to realize was that by directly challenging many of the expectations and entitlements, political and economic, nurtured during the Brezhnev era, this agenda would contribute decisively to the erosion of the remaining sources of stability in national relations.

For example, while Gorbachev lent his support to proposals for expanding the economic role and rights of republics and regions, the view that economic stringency dictated sharp cutbacks in non-essential investment, and that resource allocation to republics for social needs should be more directly linked to their performance, threatened a sharp diminution of support for those republics most heavily dependent on central allocations. The Central Asian republics, with their rapidly expanding populations and urgent need for investments in social infrastructure, were most directly threatened by this shift. Coupled with the cancellation of the Siberian river diversion project, which foreclosed the prospect of abundant new sources of water for the irrigation of cotton and other crops, these initial economic policies were a clear message that the shift from an extensive to an intensive pattern of economic development meant that Central Asia could no longer count on major investments from the centre but would have to rely far more heavily on its own internal resources.

The Gorbachev leadership's insistence on the need to restore discipline in cadres policy was equally unsettling to republic elites. The attack on Brezhnev's policy of 'trust in cadres' reflected the view that a general laxness and insufficient exactingness toward cadres had permitted the creation of republican satrapies which had effectively escaped central control. As Gorbachev put it in his political report to the Twenty-Seventh Party Congress: 'At some stage, some republics, territories, regions and cities were placed outside the boundaries of criticism'.[9] Moreover, rejecting the view that 'affirmative action' on behalf of local nationals was a legitimate consideration in personnel appointments, the new leadership harshly criticized the substitution of nepotism and favouritism for meritocratic criteria. The 'mechanical distribution of places and posts according to national criteria' was condemned as a 'vulgarization of the very idea of internationalism'.[10]

Closely allied with a highly-publicized campaign against corruption, this new cadres policy resulted in massive purges of republic and local leaderships, and their replacement, in many cases, by trusted Russians sent from the centre. These purges, and the investigations of widespread corruption which accompanied them, fell most heavily on the Central Asian elites.[11] Because of the different ways in which national elites in different parts of the country had built their political positions, the new orientations in economic policy and in cadres policy, coupled with the highly-publicized campaign against corruption, constituted an especially direct assault on the power and status of key Central Asian party and state officials.[12]

References to the need for due representation of all nationalities in the Party and government bodies of the national republics, a veiled call for increased appointments of Russians, coupled with advocacy of increasing the 'inter-republican exchange of cadres – a euphemism for a policy of assigning trusted officials from the centre to key positions in the non-Russian republics – also seemed to foreshadow a more aggressive personnel policy by the new leadership. Moreover, cadres policies which rejected the preferential recruitment of ethnic minorities into political positions implicitly favoured the appointment of ethnic Russians to key positions in the central state and party apparatus as well. Fifty of the fifty-five all-Union ministers appointed between 1985 and 1987 were Russian, as were virtually all new Politburo members.

To what extent these early policies reflected the views of Mikhail Gorbachev himself remains unclear. It may well be the case that this assertive personnel policy was primarily identified with Yegor Ligachev, who in this period had direct responsibility for cadres. Gorbachev's own speeches do *not* refer to the need to give due representation to all nationalities in party and government bodies in the national republics, nor do they call for the inter-republic exchange of cadres, while Ligachev, by contrast, strongly advocated such an approach in his speech to the Twenty-Seventh Party Congress and on other occasions. Moreover, by 1988–9, when Ligachev's influence in the leadership was considerably diminished, a major shift in personnel policy was evident. Officials appointed to the position of republic First Secretary were increasingly of the local nationality, and in some cases were figures who commanded some respect in their respective republics.

The unintended consequences of the leadership's aggressive new approaches to resource allocation and to cadres policy, however, were brought home most dramatically when, in the wake of economic policies perceived as detrimental to Central Asian interests, as well as massive purges of personnel on charges of corruption, the replacement of Dinmukhamed Kunaev, the ethnically Kazakh first secretary of the Kazakhstan party organization, by Gennadiy Kolbin, a Russian, triggered massive rioting in the capital city of Alma Ata.[13]

But the initial reformist programme encountered growing difficulties and resistance on other grounds as well, and failed to arrest a further deterioration of the economic situation. By late summer 1986, Gorbachev and some – but by no means all – of his colleagues within the leadership had come to the conclusion that economic stagnation had its roots in deeper social and political problems, and that more far-reaching changes were needed if they were to be successfully addressed. Gorbachev's growing recognition of the socio-political sources of stagnation was in turn reflected in the evolution of his conception of *perestroika*. From its initial focus on economic acceleration and tighter political controls, it now expanded to encompass, in Gorbachev's words, 'not only the economy but all other sides of social life'. This redefinition of the whole meaning of reform, which now brought political reform to the centre of attention and which assigned a critical place to *glasnost'* and democratization, would have far-reaching consequences for the national question in Soviet political life.

THE IMPACT OF *PERESTROIKA* ON THE NATIONAL QUESTION

In seeking to tap the sources of vitality, dynamism and innovation that had developed outside the framework of official institutions, Gorbachev's reforms progressively expanded the boundaries of legitimate economic, social and political activity. The changes initiated from above created novel opportunities for the emergence and mobilization of new social actors. In particular, the official endorsement of *glasnost'* and democratization significantly altered the relationship of state and society, legitimizing new forms of expression and activity, expanding the resources at the disposal of new groups, and altering the calculus of costs and benefits associated with political activism.[14] By transforming the structure of political opportunities, the reforms were the critical catalyst in mobilizing a variety of grievances and providing them with new forms of expression.

During the first three years of the Gorbachev era, from 1985 until the spring of 1988, the progressive broadening of the scope of *glasnost'* provoked an upsurge of national consciousness that extended to virtually every region of the country. The delegitimation of Stalinism, closely linked as it was to the espousal of a socialist pluralism of ideas, gave official sanction to increasingly sharp critiques of Stalinist nationality policies, or indeed, to any practices that might be so labelled. It also called into question the entire gamut of assumptions, institutions, and values that had formed the core of

Soviet nationality theory and policy over many decades, and nurtured the hope – and indeed the expectation – that long-standing grievances and injustices would now be rectified. Gorbachev's explicit acknowledgement, in the wake of mounting inter-ethnic tensions and conflicts, that Soviet scholarship had presented an excessively rosy view of Soviet achievements in national relations, his call for greater truthfulness in analyzing real problems, and his explicit support for filling in the 'blank pages' in Soviet history, were taken as authoritative permission to reopen controversial issues of nationality policy previously closed to discussion.

For example, Gorbachev's speech to the Central Committee plenum in January 1987 included an acknowledgement that the problems brought to the surface by the demonstrations of December 1986 in Alma Ata were hardly confined to Kazakhstan, that the Party had committed real errors in nationality policy, and that the taboos which prevented serious discussion of these issues only exacerbated them. Blaming scholars for presenting too complacent assessments of Soviet reality, he called upon social scientists to conduct serious analyses of nationality problems.[15] It fell to a well-known author of precisely such rosy assessments to spell out the implications of this speech for future work on Soviet nationality theory and practice. In a major article in *Pravda*, Eduard Bagramov of the Institute of Marxism-Leninism, presented an exceptionally sharp critique of key features of traditional approaches, and invited social scientists to contribute a more candid and realistic assessment.[16]

In the national republics as in Moscow, the extension of *glasnost'* to the national question opened the door to an ever-widening public discussion of highly sensitive issues, a virtual outpouring of long-suppressed resentments, and growing demands for fundamental policy changes. Under the umbrella of *glasnost'*, what had long been an Aesopian dialogue among intellectual elites was increasingly transformed into publicly-articulated demands by newly-emerging cultural and socio-political movements devoted to national revival, which adopted names like 'Awakening', 'Rebirth', and 'Revival' to convey their goals.

Out of an amorphous mixture of resentments and grievances that found growing expression in the local media, as well as at scholarly and cultural gatherings, the cultural and intellectual elites of the national republics began to elaborate an increasingly coherent critique of a whole gamut of Soviet nationality policies, based on an interpretation of the Soviet experience that directly challenged the prevailing official myths. This process of 'cognitive liberation' not only altered the whole discourse concerning national relations; it also sought to legitimize national self-assertion by identifying it with the processes of reform and democratization initiated by the party leadership itself.

With the inauguration, in the spring of 1988, of a new stage of the reform process, which centred on the democratization of political life and the introduction of competitive elections, the new intellectual currents nurtured by *glasnost'* coalesced into political programmes identified with embryonic new political movements. In the Soviet setting and the ideological vacuum resulting from the delegitimation of Stalinism and increasingly of Marxism-Leninism as well, it was predictable that these new organizations (initially unofficial and informal but over time developing into structured socio-political movements) would be overwhelmingly, although by no means exclusively, national movements. Although the emerging political configuration embraced a broad spectrum of causes and orientations, including liberal-democratic, Christian, social-democratic, monarchist, and 'green' movements, common nationality and shared historical grievances were among the most powerful of all potential bonds, and the scale of the national republics and density of ties among their intellectual elites offered a natural basis for organization.

The emergence of a new, if rudimentary, parliamentary system following the 1989 elections opened a third stage in the reform process. The elections not only gave enormous impetus to the process of political mobilization; they also had far-reaching consequences for the structure of power in the Soviet system, the role of the Communist Party, and the nature of centre-periphery relations. By compelling local party officials to become responsive to local constituencies, not only did the political reforms give unprecedented leverage to organized local groups; they also accelerated the fragmentation of the Party along national lines.[17]

Not only were party organizations of different republics increasingly at odds with each other; growing national tensions within republic party organizations, exacerbated by struggles between conservatives and reformers at the centre, were making it increasingly difficult to maintain party unity and discipline in the face of conflicting pulls. The problem became particularly acute in the Baltic republics and Moldavia, as the radicalization of the popular fronts brought increasing pressure to bear on the party organizations to back their programmes or risk losing popular support. The most dramatic challenge to party unity came in Lithuania, whose Communist Party – further emboldened by political developments in Eastern Europe – declared its independence from Moscow. As segments of the republic party leaderships formed virtual coalitions with the people's fronts, Russians and members of other non-titular nationalities in these republics expressed growing outrage at what they considered their leadership's deviation from party principles, and formed counter-movements to defend their interests.

The process of democratization was also accompanied by a progressive shift of political initiative from the Party to legislative and governmental bodies. In the republics as at the all-Union level, the newly-elected parliaments were no longer content to serve as rubber stamps; they began to view themselves as genuine arenas of public debate and policymaking, and as the vehicle for the legitimate expression of republic interests. As the political elites of the national republics emerged as major actors in the unfolding struggles over power and policy, they increasingly saw themselves as defenders of republic interests against the centre.

The election of Boris Yel'tsin to the Chairmanship of the RSFSR Supreme Soviet, and the adoption of a declaration of sovereignty by the Russian republic in May 1990, opened a fifth stage in these developments, giving both legitimacy and a powerful new impetus to the demands for a fundamental change in the nature of the Soviet federation. These pressures could no longer be ascribed to a handful of extremists or separatists in the Baltic or other non-Russian republics: they now emanated from the Russian heartland itself.

In short, *glasnost'* and democratization unleashed a simultaneous cognitive and political revolution which transformed the nature of Soviet politics and, in the process, the 'National Question'. By contributing to the erosion of the core values and institutions which had long served as the integrating forces in the Soviet multinational system, the Gorbachev reforms brought into question the entire definition of the Soviet political community and compelled a reassessment of the nature and future of the Soviet federation itself.

NEW POLITICAL THINKING ON THE NATIONAL QUESTION

By contrast with the policy debates of the Brezhnev era, the dominant challenge to traditional views of the 'National Question' now came from the advocates of greater decentralization and pluralism. The 'New Political Thinking' about nationalism and national identity called into question the central myth which had long provided the ideological underpinnings of Soviet nationality policy: the myth of internationalism itself.

The point of departure of new thinking was the explicit abandonment of the illusion that the 'National Question' could be once and for all time 'solved'. For decades, Soviet policy had been based on the expectation that modernization and socialism would automatically erode national identities and loyalties and promote the creation of a new multinational community based on the equality, prosperity, harmony and growing uniformity of its members. Such illusions were now dispelled. The focus, in Soviet rhetoric, on 'solving' (*reshenie*) the national question was increasingly replaced by a focus on 'managing' (*upravlenie*) it.

This shift went hand in hand with the growing recognition that Soviet policy had itself contributed to exacerbating national relations. Whether the problems had their roots in Stalinist distortions of Leninist principles, as the leadership maintained, or whether they derived from Lenin's own faulty approach to the issue of nationalism, as some scholars and activists alleged, the whole Soviet record was now up for reassessment.[18] This reassessment was endorsed by the Institute of Marxism-Leninism itself, which now acknowledged that its previous understanding of these issues had been incomplete and distorted.[19]

Central to this shift was the reassessment of the federal system itself. Article after article now proclaimed that the Soviet Union was in fact a highly-centralized, virtually unitary state disguised in the trappings of a federation; its republics, insisted one historian, enjoyed less autonomy than had the provinces of the Tsarist empire.

Glasnost' also opened public discussion of the circumstances in which various republics had joined the USSR, rekindling controversies over boundaries and territorial claims as well as over the nature of the federal system.[20] Some of these discussions were directed at Russian imperial expansion; Central Asian historians, for example, demanded a more truthful accounting of the process of forcible conquest which had brought the region under the control of the Tsarist government.[21] Other debates involved longstanding animosities or conflicts among non-Russians.

The most sustained and bitter struggle over historical rectification – a struggle with unmistakable political implications – was conducted by elites and activists in the three Baltic republics to force the Soviet leadership to publicly acknowledge the secret protocol of the Molotov–Ribbentrop Pact of 1939 and its role in paving the way for the forcible Soviet annexation of Latvia, Lithuania, and Estonia during the Second World War. The campaign initially met with the standard official denials, as leading officials in Moscow asserted that the existence of the alleged protocol – whose full text was published for the first time in the Soviet Union in the Estonian language in 1988 – could not be proven as no original documents could be found. A series of articles, conferences, and reports in the Baltic media documenting the events of 1939 in rich detail eventually paved the way for the creation of a special commission of the newly-elected Supreme Soviet to examine the question. In August 1989, in an effort to preempt the findings of the commission as well as planned commemorations of the event in the Baltic republics, the Soviet leadership was compelled to acknowledge the signing of the secret protocol; and the subsequent revision of it. But it continued to deny that there was any connection between the protocol and the subsequent accession of the Baltic republics to the USSR, and insisted that the entire agreement had been voided in any case by the German attack on the USSR in 1941.

In the fierce debates that now raged over nationality policy countless other long-standing assumptions came under attack. The notion that the Soviet socialist system had destroyed all vestiges of the tsarist 'prison of nations' was challenged by the argument that the USSR was an empire even more oppressive than its predecessor. The myth that socialism had promoted economic equality among nations was supplanted by a bitter argument over who was exploiting whom. The very notion of Russians as benevolent 'elder brothers' was attacked as a patronizing effort to disguise the reality of Russification and assimilation. Russians themselves began to complain with growing bitterness of this unprecedented and unjustified wave of Russophobia.

Another important feature of the new thinking about nationality issues was the novel value now attached to national distinctiveness. In an environment newly hospitable to the idea of pluralism, the traditional view that *sliyanie* – the convergence and ultimate fusion of nations and nationalities – was both a possible and a desirable goal of Soviet policy came under explicit attack. The disappearance of national diversity, it was now argued, would constitute an irreparable human loss.[22] Gorbachev himself expressed concern for national values in affirming, in January 1989, that ' . . . we cannot permit even the smallest people to disappear, the language of even the smallest people to be lost; we cannot permit nihilism with regard to the culture, traditions and history of peoples, be they big or small'.[23]

The new concern with rediscovering, reviving, and protecting national groups and their cultural heritage not only repudiated earlier assimilationist goals; it attached new importance to the revival of national languages and cultures, and to the role of the national republics as a framework for defending national values and identities. During the Brezhnev era, advocates of circumscribing the powers of the republics, if not eliminating them altogether, were on the offensive. Now that the republics were emerging as major political actors as a consequence of *perestroika* this position – while retaining powerful adherents – could no longer go unchallenged.

Indeed, one striking and novel element of this 'New Thinking' was the emergence of a specifically *Russian* national consciousness, focused on the demand for the creation of Russian republic institutions. Where previously Russian nationalism had been closely identified with imperial aspirations, and had treated the preservation of centralized Soviet power as a primary goal, this new strain aspired to the creation of a Russian nation-state as an equal partner in a reconstructed Soviet federation of sovereign republics.

The major dilemma raised by this new thinking on nations and nationalism, and a dilemma which proved exceptionally divisive for reformers, was how to address the conflicting claims for national self-determination by the Union republics and by sub-republic minorities. The Inter-Regional Group, influenced by the views of Andrey Sakharov and Galina Staravoytova, tended toward the position that only by giving equal recognition to all claims for national self-determination could the invidious hierarchical structure of national groups established by Soviet rule be overcome. Other reformers, however, feared that this approach, by weakening the rights of the Union republics, played into the hands of the centre. In their view measures to enhance the rights of national minorities (such as the Law on Secession adopted by the Supreme Soviet on 3 April 1990, which permitted autonomous republics and even 'compact national groups' to hold separate referendums on secession) were designed to thwart in practice the right of national self-determination of the titular nationality of the republic.[24]

A final element in the emerging new thinking about national relations was the repudiation of a striving for uniformity. Insisting that a country as vast and diverse as the USSR could not be treated as a monolithic whole, with uniform policies laid down by an omnipotent centre, reformers called for the formulation of differentiated policies suited to the distinctive features and needs of different regions of the country. The radical decentralization of decision-making they advocated would in any case result in increasingly diverse patterns of economic, political and cultural life from republic to republic; in different kinds of ties between centre and periphery; and in new relationships between republics and countries outside their borders. How, and even whether, these variations could be accommodated within the framework of a single political, economic and legal universe now emerged as a major topic of controversy.

Underlying the struggles between traditional and reformist assumptions about nations and national identity were two contending visions of the Soviet future itself. Reformers argued that the USSR should be reconstructed as a genuine federation, or even confederation, of sovereign national republics which should enjoy substantial economic and political autonomy in shaping the destiny of their historical homelands.[25] The centre, in their view, should carry out only those limited functions of foreign and security policy, and of overall economic coordination, delegated by the republics.[26] Conservatives, although giving lip service to reform of the federal system, assigned highest priority to preserving the Union and were fundamentally hostile to what they viewed as dangerous centrifugal forces. They viewed the entire territory of the Soviet Union as 'our common home', argued – by analogy with the American model – that the individual rather than the national group was the proper subject of political rights,[27] and insisted there should be no corner of Soviet territory in which a Soviet citizen could not feel at home. The Gorbachev leadership, bitterly divided by these issues, struggled to find a position between the two around which a centrist consensus could be sustained.

THE EVOLUTION OF GORBACHEV'S VIEWS OF THE NATIONAL QUESTION

As we have argued, the Soviet leadership, and Gorbachev in particular, had failed to anticipate that this entire process of reform would reignite the 'National Question', and they underestimated its potential explosiveness. In this as in other areas, Gorbachev's education was a rapid one; in two short years, between 1986 and 1988, swiftly moving events not only propelled what at first seemed an irrelevant issue to the top of the Soviet political agenda but radically transformed the leadership's understanding of it.[28] By 1989 Gorbachev had come to realize that the 'National Question' was inescapably entwined with reform, and a restructuring of national relations was explicitly incorporated into the reform agenda. One year later, he was struggling to cope no longer with reform but with revolution. Even the National Question had been superseded – by the question of the future of the Union itself!

Gorbachev would surely look back with irony on a speech he had delivered in Lithuania in June 1980 to mark the fortieth anniversary of its annexation to the Soviet Union. Entitled 'Friendship of USSR Peoples – An Invaluable Achievement', the speech is permeated with the official complacency and self-congratulation that was a hallmark of the Brezhnev era. Even after his accession to power, Gorbachev's expressed views on the subject still conveyed the traditional platitudes. In his speech of 8 May 1985 to mark the fortieth anniversary of Soviet victory in the Second World War Gorbachev affirmed that 'the blossoming of nations and nationalities is organically connected to their all-round drawing together. Into the consciousness and heart of every person there has deeply entered the feeling of belonging to a single family – the Soviet people, a new and historically unprecedented social and international community'.[29]

Over the next four years, in response to the growing tide of national self-assertion across the USSR, Gorbachev's pronouncements on nationality policy underwent a radical change. The distance he had travelled is most dramatically evident if the optimism of these early speeches is compared with the sombre address he delivered on nationwide television on 1 July 1989 in the wake of mounting ethnic violence in Soviet Central Asia. Expressing alarm at the 'tremendous danger' posed by growing national tensions and conflict, both to the fate of *perestroika* and to the integrity of the Soviet state, he warned that those who fanned such strife were 'playing with fire'. 'The present generation and our descendants', he asserted, 'will curse both those who pushed us onto this path and those who did not warn in time and stop the madness'.[30]

Gorbachev's evolution reflected both a broader process of learning about the scope and depth of his country's problems and a major shift in political strategy. His statements reveal a steadily growing awareness that national relations in the USSR were far more conflictual and problematic than he had previously realized. They present an increasingly harsh assessment of the assumptions and policies that had aggravated them. They express a growing sensitivity to the grievances of national elites and a recognition that some accommodation to their demands was essential to the future of *perestroika* itself. But they stop short of sanctioning a significant devolution of power to the republics.

The change in Gorbachev's underlying assumptions was accompanied by a shift in policy as well. From an initial approach to reform which largely ignored the national question, it is possible to trace the gradual development of a political strategy which made a fundamental restructuring of the Soviet federal system – including new mechanisms for dealing with inter-ethnic relations – a key component of the reform programme. Both learning and policy change were in turn a reaction to rapidly-unfolding events which made it clear that political coalition-building on behalf of reform could not be based exclusively on his original economic and political agenda, but had to accommodate the national aspirations of key republic as well as central elites. By 1989, a *perestroika* of national relations had moved to the top of Gorbachev's political agenda.

None of this was anticipated when Gorbachev succeeded to the Soviet political leadership. During his first months as General Secretary, Gorbachev gave no indication that nationality policy was part of the reform agenda, or that it was itself in need of reassessment. As he would later confess, the leadership initially underestimated the urgency of the entire issue:

> It must be admitted that at the beginning of restructuring we by no means fully appreciated the need for updating nationalities policy. Probably we were too slow in resolving a number of urgent questions. Meanwhile, natural dissatisfaction with the economic and social problems that had accumulated began to be perceived as an infringement on national interests . . . .[31]

Even before his accession, as we have seen, Gorbachev had revealed himself to be a strong advocate of political and economic rationalization and a proponent of shifting from an extensive to an intensive pattern of economic development. Economic reform was the prism through which he viewed other issues, and efficiency rather than equity was his primary focus. When he addressed problems of centre–periphery relations, it was primarily from the standpoint of how the republics might more effectively contribute to the development of a single, unified national economic complex. Gorbachev's speech on ideology at an all-Union conference in December 1984, for example, typically gave priority to the need for 'a rational distribution of productive forces and their further integration into the overall national economic complex', just as his remarks at the Twenty-Seventh Party Congress in February 1986 expressed impatience with the parasitic attitude of some republics which sought to live, in effect, at the expense of the rest, and to promote local interests without making an appropriate contribution to the welfare of the Union as a whole. If Gorbachev's views on economic and personnel matters gave primacy to considerations of efficiency over entitlements, and of integration over decentralization, his views on nationality theory – while relatively sparse – were comparatively enlightened. They were largely free, for example, of the patronizing attitude toward non-Russians reflected in ritual references to the debt of gratitude owed to the Russians for their sacrifices on behalf of others, a staple of Brezhnev's speeches on the subject. They also avoided any hint that progress toward socialism would facilitate the gradual merger (*sliyanie*) of nations and nationalities. Indeed, Gorbachev himself acknowledged that during the preparation of the party programme in 1985, he personally had opposed proposals by 'certain learned gentlemen' to incorporate in the programme the 'dangerous formulation' about the 'merging of nations' which Andropov himself had once endorsed.[32]

Gorbachev's political report to the Twenty-Seventh Party Congress, on 25 February 1986, like his later statements, was similarly free of the Russo-centric thrust characteristic of Brezhnev's pronouncements. The nationality issue occupied only a marginal place in his lengthy report, another indication of its marginal claim on his attention, and primarily in the context of economic policy. While Gorbachev took a favourable view of expanding the economic role of republic and local organs in order to strengthen the territorial aspects of economic planning and management, he warned yet again of the dangers of localism and of parasitism, and stressed once more the importance of linking resource allocation to the efficiency of each republic. Finally, his remarks treated the growing interest in national heritage and roots as a healthy and desirable phenomenon, while at the same time warning against the tendency toward self-isolation.[33] They acknowledged that 'contradictions are inherent in any development, and they are inevitable in this sphere as well' and stressed, in an almost routine way, the need for special sensitivity and circumspection in dealing with national issues.

These 'contradictions' became increasingly visible over the course of the next few years. The demonstrations in Alma Ata in December 1986 were the first in a series of jolts that would transform the Soviet leadership's view of nationality relations from complacency to alarm. Gorbachev's speech to the Central Committee plenum in January 1987 included an acknowledgement that the problems brought to the surface by the Alma Ata demonstrations extended far beyond Kazakhstan. He admitted that the Party had committed real mistakes in nationality policy, and that the taboos which had prevented serious discussion of these problems had only served to aggravate them. Blaming scholars for excessively rosy assessments of Soviet reality – rather unfairly, given the enormous ideological constraints and bureaucratic pressures on Soviet social science – he called on Soviet social scientists to stop depicting national relations in terms 'more reminiscent of complimentary toasts rather than of serious scientific studies'.[34] Gorbachev's recognition of the limitations of existing Soviet scholarship, and his call for serious scholarly analyses of nationality problems was an open invitation to extend the scope of *glasnost'* to this domain. It was quickly taken up by scholars in the national republics as well as in Moscow.

In subsequent months the first, tentative airings of grievances encouraged by *glasnost'* mushroomed into increasingly sharp discussions, escalating demands, public demonstrations of growing frequency and scale, and increasingly organized protest. Gorbachev himself was directly exposed to the rising current of national feeling when he visited Estonia and Latvia in the spring of 1987. In conversations with workers as well as cultural figures, he admitted that the Baltic republics' road to socialism had been thorny and complex, and acknowledged 'omissions' and 'miscalculations' in party policy.

By the summer of 1987, the leadership found itself faced with a mounting wave of anti-Russian demonstrations in the Baltic, which reached a crescendo on the anniversary of the Molotov–Ribbentrop Pact on 23 August. Even Red Square became the scene of demonstrations for national rights: in July 1987 Crimean Tatars assembled there to demand the restoration of their homeland. Less dramatic and publicly visible, but also of concern, were the growing expressions of grievances over language and cultural policy in a number of republics, and of environmental protests given new impetus by the catastrophe at Chernobyl'.

In the autumn of 1987, still seeking to assimilate the lessons of Alma Ata and of continuing manifestations of national unrest, the Gorbachev leadership issued its first major statement on national relations. In an editorial in the Party's ideological journal, *Kommunist*, the conventional clichés about the achievements of socialism in resolving the nationality problem were joined to a novel acknowledgement that 'negative manifestations' like nationalism, chauvinism, and localism might have deep structural roots.[35] Further, while the article deplored the inadequacies of Soviet social science in addressing nationality problems, it acknowledged that it would have been 'unpleasant' to have spoken frankly, in earlier times, of mistakes. Finally, amidst the conventional and unpromising list of policy recommendations there appeared, alongside the usual exhortation to strengthen training in the Russian language, a reference to the need for improving the teaching of national languages in Russian schools.

While it announced no major new departures in either theory or practice, the editorial reflected the broader impact of *glasnost'* on the treatment of nationality problems. By endorsing and encouraging a more frank acknowledgement of real problems, and criticizing the long-standing tendency to exaggerate Soviet achievements while sweeping problems under the carpet, it licensed more extensive reassessments of the issues and more radical critiques of traditional practices, both at the centre and in the national republics.

By the end of 1987, the leadership's earlier view of the nationalities question as marginal was giving way to a recognition that it was becoming an increasingly important locus of political problems. In a speech marking the seventieth anniversary of the October Revolution, Gorbachev indicated that *perestroika* and democratization were having important consequences for national relations, and that the Party intended to address the issue in greater depth in the near future. These plans had crystallized, by early 1988, into a decision to devote a special plenum of the Party's Central Committee to the issue, to be convened in the autumn. In a striking demonstration of how far his own views had evolved under the pressure of events, Gorbachev now identified nationalities policy as 'the most fundamental, vital issue of our society' and called for a thorough review of both theory and practice.[36]

In the summer of 1988 the Soviet leadership confronted the worst crisis yet in national relations. Long-standing Armenian claims to Nagorno-Karabakh, an autonomous enclave within the Azerbaijan SSR populated largely by Armenians, escalated into massive demonstrations in both Armenia and Nagorno-Karabakh, demanding the territory's transfer to the Armenian Republic. Provoked by this threat to the territorial integrity of their republic, Azeris responded with counter-demonstrations and escalating violence that culminated in a massacre of Armenian residents in Sumgait.

The conflict over Nagorno-Karabakh highlighted the political dilemmas created by the Soviet leadership's endorsement of democratization, as well as its efforts to redress some of the crimes of the Stalin era. Moscow's posture encouraged Armenian expectations that past violations of their rights would be rectified, which would inevitably have created a confrontation with Azerbaijan. Caught in what was essentially a zero-sum situation, with violence escalating on both sides, Gorbachev concluded that no satisfactory solution could be found and – at the cost of alienating both sides – he placed the territory under direct rule from the centre. The eruption and escalation of the Karabakh crisis dramatically highlighted the extent to which, here as in other areas, developments on the ground were themselves beginning to drive policy. The Soviet leadership increasingly found itself in the position of reacting – too slowly and not always wisely – to events it could no longer fully direct or control, and the instruments at its disposal for managing rising inter-ethnic tensions and conflicts appeared increasingly inadequate to the task.

By the time the Nineteenth Party Conference met in June 1988, and endorsed plans for a Central Committee plenum on national relations, it was clear that a major reconsideration of the whole framework of nationality policy was necessary. Not only did the Party face growing demands for changes in language and cultural policies; for border rectifications, and for increased economic autonomy; serious clashes among national groups were becoming a growing danger. Furthermore, the broader political reforms under discussion, including a proposed reorganization of the USSR Supreme Soviet, would have important consequences for the way in which republic and nationality interests would be represented.

In his speech to the Conference Gorbachev went a step further than previously in acknowledging that questions involving the treatment of national languages, cultures, history, historical monuments and the environment had been neglected in the past, and that nationalist excesses were in many cases a result of the failure to respond to emerging needs in a timely way. But his remarks also reflected the increasing gravity of the situation: preserving the unity of the peoples of the USSR, and harmonizing the interests of each nation with the concerns of the larger Soviet community, could no longer be taken for granted. It had become the central issue.

It was only at the Central Committee plenum held in July 1988 that

the broad agenda for the meeting on relations between nationalities
was finally published, and that the leadership's current views on the
subject were spelled out at some length. Seeking to explain the
reasons for the exacerbation of inter-ethnic relations, Gorbachev's
remarks were more sharply critical of past practices than ever before.
While singling out inattention, over many years, to the specific social,
economic, and spiritual needs of the nations and nationalities of the
country, and abuse of power by officials in conditions of insufficient
accountability to the population, Gorbachev's acknowledgement of
past errors was joined to the accusation – one he would return to
repeatedly – that corrupt groups were manipulating and exploiting
national conflicts to impede the process of restructuring.[37] Gorbachev
proposed to deal with the latter by increasing the penalties for
preaching racial or national exclusiveness, or fanning national dis-
cord.

The most notable feature of Gorbachev's speech was its unusually
sympathetic treatment of national–cultural needs, an ever-sharper
departure from earlier attitudes:

> I do not have to talk about how attentive we must be to the
> development of native languages and national cultures, to environ-
> mental protection and historical monuments, and to everything
> that defines the uniqueness of each nation and nationality and its
> inimitable contribution to the general treasure-house of Soviet
> culture, which is characterized by its multifaceted nature and a
> polychromatic picture of national colours.[38]

The sweeping agenda for the forthcoming plenum outlined in Gorbachev's speech, and incorporated in the conference resolution 'On
Relations Between Nationalities', made it clear that the leadership
was now prepared to contemplate a significant set of changes in
Soviet nationality policy.[39] Responding to the broad array of grievances and demands emanating from republic elites, emerging socio-
political groups, and writers and scholars, as well as to the specific
crises with which it found itself grappling, the leadership proposed a
broad framework for restructuring nationality policies along more
permissive lines. It embraced the structure of the Soviet federal
system itself, including a demarcation of the jurisdictions of the
centre and the republics, and promised a considerable expansion of
the powers of the republics. It called for important changes in
language and cultural policy, including support for expanding the

role of national languages within the republics. It also directed particular attention to the needs and grievances of nationalities living outside their 'own' republics or lacking them, presumably a gesture in the direction of Russian settler communities as well as indigenous minority groups.

The need for far-reaching changes was justified, in the resolution, by the argument that in the course of Soviet history Leninist principles of nationalities policy had been progressively undermined, and acute problems were ignored or repressed. The task ahead was to cleanse Leninist norms of all 'artificial encrustations and deformations'. Acknowledging that 'present-day nationalities policy needs thoroughgoing scientific and theoretical elaboration', the resolution called on specialists to pool their efforts in this undertaking and proposed that consideration be given to establishing a national research centre devoted to the study of national relations.[40]

These decisions can be taken as a renunciation, by the party leadership, of any remaining illusions about the scope and depth of inter-ethnic tensions, and a recognition of the serious challenges the situation posed. As Gorbachev put it in a grave speech to the Supreme Soviet in November 1988:

> Restructuring has literally blown up the illusory peace and harmony that reigned in our country during the years of stagnation, has given impetus to wide-ranging and unrestricted debate, and has brought many urgent and even painful questions to the surface. It is necessary that the enormous energy of this social process not be dissipated or squandered to no purpose, and especially that it not take the shape of social and national strife, but that it be applied to realistic undertakings and directed wholly toward the achievement of truly revolutionary, constructive goals. We are now confronted by immense and complicated tasks. It is important not to lose heart when faced with the scope of innovation or with the diversity of the opinion and emotions that have spilled forth.[41]

The significance of these decisions also lay in the fact that a restructuring of national relations was now explicitly incorporated into the agenda of political reforms.[42] Their adoption marked an important further step in recognizing the scope and seriousness of the problems and their destructive potential, and in contemplating more far-reaching measures to address them. As Gorbachev put it, the Party had come to recognize that 'the success of restructuring will depend to a decisive extent' on how the problems that had accumulated in nationality relations were handled.[43]

But events would once again move far ahead of the leadership's ability to shape them. The spring and summer of 1989 were marked by a further escalation of national tensions: the increasing political assertiveness of national movements in a number of republics, including the growth of explicitly separatist tendencies; the tragic attempt at repression by military forces of a non-violent demonstration in Tbilisi on 9 April which resulted in the death of sixteen civilians and produced a wave of bitterness directed against Moscow; a virtual civil war over Nagorno-Karabakh which Moscow appeared unable to control and which resulted in a massive wave of refugees; and outbreaks of terrifying violence against ethnic minorities in Uzbekistan and Kazakhstan. In an urgent appeal to his people on nationwide television, Gorbachev voiced what had by now become the ultimate nightmare: 'What if inter-ethnic strife spreads and embraces regions where millions of people of other nationalities live alongside people of the indigenous nationality?'[44]

As the party leadership prepared for the long-awaited and much-postponed Central Committee plenum, it confronted yet one additional crisis. On 23 August, the fiftieth anniversary of the signing of the Molotov–Ribbentrop Pact was marked by the formation of a human chain across the three Baltic republics to protest against Soviet annexation of the region, which had just been declared illegal by a special commission of the Lithuanian Supreme Soviet. Responding to this overt challenge to the territorial integrity of the Soviet state, and to the legitimacy of Soviet power, the Central Committee issued a harsh denunciation of the 'national hysteria' that had infested the Baltic region like a virus and warned ominously that 'the fate of the Baltic peoples is in serious danger'.[45]

The crisis in the Baltic republics, which culminated in Lithuania's declaration of the independence and the institution of a blockade against the republic, reflected in microcosm the fundamental dilemma of the Gorbachev reforms. To deal effectively with the country's problems, the leadership was forced to progressively distance itself from important features of previous assumptions and policies. By its own behaviour, however, it had unwittingly unleashed and encouraged at the grassroots level new forms of sociopolitical mobilization around national issues that could not readily be accommodated within the existing structure of power. The effort to encourage the process of democratization, while at the same time rejecting the demands for genuine self-determination which were its outcome, or to support a restructuring of the federation without acquiescing in the transfer of significant powers and resources to the republics, placed Gorbachev yet once more in the role, as one commentator put it, of both Luther and the Pope, and alienated reformers and conservatives alike.

Both the extent of Gorbachev's evolution on the 'National Question' and the limits to his 'New Thinking' on the issue, were most dramatically revealed in the struggle to frame a new Union Treaty.[46] Having established the Council of the Federation, a new government advisory body composed of representatives of the fifteen Union republics, he left the preparation of the draft document to the central party and state apparatus with only ritual consultation with republic authorities. Predictably, the resulting draft – which adopted the language of republic sovereignty but in fact provided for a relatively limited devolution of powers by the centre to the republics – failed to satisfy their demands. At the same time, Gorbachev launched a harsh attack on a competing approach favoured by Yel'tsin and embodied in the Shatalin 'Five Hundred Days Plan'. The product of direct horizontal consultations among republics, it proposed to restructure the federation along the lines of the European Community, with the sovereign republics delegating to the centre only those powers necessary to the pursuit of common economic, foreign policy and security goals. Charging his opponents with advocating the disintegration and 'Lebanonization' of the USSR, Gorbachev called on the Communist Party to struggle against nationalist and separatist forces in favour of integration in 'up-to-date forms'.[47]

In struggling to preserve the key functions and powers of the centre, and to resist the mounting pressures for a more radical devolution of power and resources to the republics, Gorbachev has been searching for new formulae with which to legitimate the preservation of a highly centralized, if no longer omnipotent Union. Faced with the challenge from the Baltic republics, he initially sought to head off pressures for independence by appealing to economic self-interest, providing elaborate statistics intended to demonstrate the dependence of each republic on the others. As economic disintegration and spreading economic autarchy weakened the argument, and gave additional impetus to the quest for foreign partners, markets, and supplies, Gorbachev has argued that the potential benefits of enhanced economic ties with the West depend on political stability and predictability, the preservation of a single national market, and the undisputed authority of a single central government. Foreign businessmen, he has warned, will turn away from economic dealings with a multiplicity of warring authorities. In recent months, Gorbachev has also given increased emphasis to the need for a strong central authority to maintain law and order. Ignoring charges that the central government has either failed to deal effectively with communal violence, as in the case of Nagorno-Karabakh and the continuing blockade of Armenia, or has contributed to it, in the case of Tbilisi, Gorbachev has warned that any weakening of the centre's powers invites escalating violence and bloodshed. Indeed, he has held out the prospect – presumably for foreign as well as domestic audiences – that the dispersion of military forces, including nuclear forces, would be a consequence of any serious redistribution of power, notwithstanding the fact that no republics to date have demanded control over nuclear forces and several have explicitly declared their desire to become nuclear-free zones. Finally, Gorbachev has emphasized that the preservation of Soviet territorial integrity and centralized power is essential if the Soviet Union is to be an active and reliable partner in building a new international system; implicitly asking Western powers to resist appeals for diplomatic support or recognition from a number of republics, and hinting that support for his position is essential to guaranteeing continuing Soviet cooperation in the international arena.

CONCLUSION

Since 1985 the Soviet rhetoric dealing with the national question and the federation, and presumably the thinking behind it, have changed dramatically. The emergence of new thinking about nationality relations and the future of the Union has largely been driven by events. With the removal of the old taboos, a broad and diverse spectrum of views now finds expression in central and local media.

Today one observes in the intense and ubiquitous Soviet arguments over these issues a diversity of discourses and metaphors which are closely linked to different political outcomes. There is, first of all, the treatment of the Soviet Union – and of tsarist Russia as an empire. This image sanctions – it virtually demands – a dissolution of empire, a break-up of the Union, and recognition of national self-determination and multiple sovereignties, possibly linked in a new form of confederation or commonwealth.

Secondly, there is the image of the USSR as a multinational state, with a stress on the organic unity of the living body, which cannot be allowed to be wrenched apart by extremists. The experience of the American Civil War is conjured up to argue the inadmissability of secession in a modern state.

A third discourse draws on the language of older Soviet concepts of a union of sovereign states but insists that they must be given greater reality. Here the implication is continued integration, but now argued largely in rational–functional terms. The ideological clichés of the past have been replaced by a discourse that refers to contemporary global economic and political trends to justify integration, and that draws on the experience of other federal systems for the design of new legal and institutional arrangements.

These are, needless to say, issues of a complexity that would be difficult either to manage or to conceptualize under the best of circumstances. But these have not been the best of circumstances for Soviet thinkers or decision-makers. 'New Thinking' has been made more difficult by conditions of economic crisis, a breakdown of political institutions and authority, and an overload of demands on the political leadership. Under the circumstances, reality is apt to diverge from the prescriptions of theorists and practitioners alike.

Notes

1. Research and interviews for this article were supported in part by a grant from the International Research and Exchanges Board (IREX), with funds provided by the National Endowment for the Humanities and the United States Information Agency. I should also like to express my appreciation to the Carnegie Corporation for its support of the larger research project of which this study is a part. None of these organizations is responsible for the views expressed.
2. See Grey Hodnett, 'What's In a Nation?', *Problems of Communism*, vol. 16 (1967), no. 5, pp. 458–81.
3. For several examples of new approaches, see U. V. Arutyunyan, 'Konkretno-sotsiologicheskoe issledovanie natsional'nykh otnoshenii', *Voprosy filosofii*, no. 12, 1969, and *Sotsial'noe i natsional'noe* (Moscow, 1973); L. M. Drobizheva, *Dukhovnaya obshchnost' narodov SSSR* (Moscow, 1981); G. Staravoyteva, 'K issledovaniyu etnopsikhologii gorodskikh zhitelei', *Sovetskaya etnografia*, no. 3, 1976; Y. V. Bromley (ed.), *Sovremennye etnicheskie protsessy v SSSR*, 2nd edn (Moscow, 1977); and V. Kozlov, *Natsional'nosti SSSR* (Moscow, 1982). A more

extended treatment of this literature is presented in the author's forth-coming *Eroding Empire: Nationalism and the Soviet Future*.

4. I. I. Krupnik, 'Mnogonatsional'noe obshchestvo (Sostoyanie natsional'-nykh otnoshenii v SSSR i zadachi nauki)', *Sovetskaya etnografia*, no. 1, 1989, pp. 53–4. For a broader treatment of these constraints, see Alexander Dallin and Bertrand Patenaude (eds), *Soviet Scholarship under Gorbachev* (Stanford CREES, 1988).

5. These dabates are treated at greater length by the author in 'Ethnonationalism and Political Stability: The Soviet Case', *World Politics*, no. 4, July 1984; and 'The Nationality Problem and The Soviet System', in Erik Hoffmann (ed.), *The Soviet Union in the 1980s* (The Academy of Political Science, 1984).

6. *Pravda*, December 1982.

7. R. I. Kosolapov, 'Klassovye i natsional'nye otnosheniya na etape razvitogo sotsialisma', *Sotsiologicheskie issledovaniya*, no. 4, 1982, p. 10. These views were also presented at a major conference in Riga in June 1982, on 'The Development of National Relations in Conditions of Developed Socialism'.

8. Ibid.

9. *Pravda*, 26 February 1986.

10. *Pravda*, 28 January 1987.

11. Major personnel shake-ups took place throughout the region from 1985 to 1987. The first party secretaries of Kirgizia, Tadzhikistan and Turkmenistan were replaced in late 1985, as were the heads of several republic KGB organizations. More than half of all Central Committee members of the Central Asian parties were ousted, with the figure reaching 80 per cent in Uzbekistan. Continuing investigations of corruption were accompanied by a media campaign exposing the crimes of local leaders.

12. Mark Beissinger, 'Ethnicity, the Personnel Weapon, and Neo-Imperial Integration: Ukrainian and RSFSR Provincial Party Officials Compared', *Studies in Comparative Communism XXI*, no. 1, Spring 1988, pp. 71–85.

13. Although accounts of these demonstrations vary, it appears that several thousand demonstrators, many of them university students and young people, took to the streets shouting 'Kazakhstan is only for Kazakhs', and broke into the local party headquarters as well as two prisons. Troops with armoured cars occupied the university and the riots were finally put down by detachments of the Ministry of Internal Affairs. At least 2000 young people were subsequently punished for their involvement in the riots, including 271 who were expelled from educational institutions and 787 from the Komsomol (*Komsomol'skaya Pravda*, 18 July 1987). See also Michel Tatu, 'Les dérapages de la Russification', *Le Monde*, 21–2 December 1986, p. 1.

14. For a more extended treatment, see Gail W. Lapidus, 'State and Society: Toward the Emergence of Civil Society in the USSR', in S. Bialer (ed.), *Politics, Society and Nationality Inside Gorbachev's Russia* (Boulder: Westview Press, 1989).

15. *Pravda*, 28 January 1987.

16. *Pravda*, 14 August 1987.

17. The dilemma of maintaining central control over local party officials while encouraging them to be responsive to local constituencies was exemplified during the dispute over Nagorno-Karabakh: in June 1988 virtually the ent..e leadership of the Armenian republic supported the transfer of Nagorno-Karabakh to Armenia, while the Azerbaijani leadership voted to retain the territory.

18. See, for example, G. I. Kunitsyn, 'Samoopredelenie natsii – istoria voprosa i sovemennost", *Voprosy filosofii* no. 9, 1988, and no. 5, 1989, pp. 66–86; K. Hallik, *Natsional'nye otnoshenia v SSSR i problemy perestroiki* (Tallinn, 1988); A. P. Nenarokov, *Za svobodnyi soyuz svobodnykh narodov* (Moscow, 1989).

19. Interviews by the author, May and August 1989.

20. It encouraged Armenian elites to reassert their claim to Nagorno-Karabakh on the grounds that Stalin had arbitrarily violated agreements which assigned the territory to Armenia; it prompted Moldavian activists to reclaim the areas of Bukovina transferred to the Ukrainian SSR during the Second World War. In short it revived innumerable territorial conflicts throughout Soviet territory that had lain dormant in more repressive times.

21. See, for example, the discussions at the meeting of the Kirgiz Writers' Union, on 23 June 1988; and of the Uzbek Writers' Union, on 24 June 1988; RL 309/88, 12 July 1988.

22. See, for example, the argument by a distinguished Soviet ethnographer, Sergey Arutyunov, that 'any disappearance of an ethnos is a tragic phenomenon . . . The concept of ethnic pluralism should have its communist variant. . . .' ('Natsional'nye protsessii v SSSR', *Istoria SSSR*, no. 6, 1987, p. 94). The most eloquent statement of this newly legitimate view by a leading political figure came in an address to a Central Committee plenum by Vaino Valjas, First Secretary of the Estonian Communist Party, who argued that the nation is the basic form of human existence, and that national culture is the foundation of universal human values (*Pravda*, 21 September 1989).

23. *Pravda*, 8 January 1989.

24. 'Yuridicheskaya literatura', *Novye zakony SSSR*, Vypusk 1, Moscow, 1990, pp. 83–90.

25. Reformers were sharply disagreed whether the fifteen Union republics alone should enjoy the right of national self-determination, or whether it should extend to autonomous republics and regions as well.

26. The reformers were themselves divided over these issues. Some reformist leaders, most notably Yel'tsin and Afanas'ev, supported the right of national self-determination even to the point of secession, while others feared it would jeopardize *perestroika* itself. Reform-minded economists such as Abalkin feared the fragmentation of a national market, and many believed that national tensions were largely the consequence of economic deterioration, and would be sharply reduced by successful economic reform.

27. The relationship of human rights to national rights was a difficult issue across the Soviet political spectrum; reformers concerned with protecting and enlarging human rights were themselves concerned with the danger

that newly-empowered national groups would threaten the rights of minorities.

28. The analysis of Gorbachev's approach to the nationality problem offered here is sharply at variance with that of Jerry Hough's 'Gorbachev's Politics', *Foreign Affairs*, Winter 1989–90, pp. 37–41. It does not support Hough's assertion that Gorbachev approached the issue with full knowledge and appreciation of the potentially explosive force of nationalism in the non-Russian republics from the beginning; that Gorbachev's behaviour reflected a coherent and well-developed strategy of deliberately utilizing inter-ethnic tensions to maintain the support of the Russian population; and that his 'policy of controlled chaos' was in fact a policy, reflecting a real capacity to control events, rather than the moves of a shrewd tactician largely reacting to events he is unable to control.

29. M. S. Gorbachev, *Izbrannye rechi i stat'i* (Moscow: Izdatel'stvo politicheskoi literatury, 1985), p. 52.

30. *Pravda*, 2 July 1989.

31. Political Report to the Supreme Soviet, *Pravda*, 31 May 1989.

32. *Pravda*, 8 January 1989. The new edition of the party programme also omitted any reference to the special role of the Russian people, or to the former 'backwardness' of other peoples of the Soviet Union, a major step forward in sensitivity.

33. His remarks affirmed that 'a healthy interest in everything that is valuable in each national culture should not degenerate into attempts to fence oneself off from the objective processes of the interaction and convergence of national cultures'.

34. *Pravda*, 28 January 1987. Gorbachev's own effort to come to grips with the contradictory aspects of national consciousness, and his lack of a firm grasp of the problem, is revealingly displayed in his remarks at a gathering with journalists the following month.

> On the one hand [he acknowledged] the cultural level of all peoples and nationalities, even the smallest, is rising, and they have developed their own intelligentsias. They study the roots of their origins, and sometimes this leads to the worshipping of history and everything connected with it, not just the progressive elements. On the other hand, new generations are entering life, and they must be reared and given up-to-date notions concerning where they live and how this highly unique phenomenon in human history was established, one in which more than a hundred nations and nationalities live – judging even by the long yardsticks of history – harmoniously and well. Nevertheless, this is real life, movement, development, and thus every stage may have its own contradictions. We must deal with this calmly, study it, decide things, and educate people. The only correct approach here is the Leninist nationalities policy, the Leninist spirit. . ..
> (*Pravda*, 14 February 1987)

He went a step further in July in affirming that 'every people has its own language and its own history; it wants to understand its roots. Can this be at variance with socialism? Of course not'. (*Pravda*, 15 July 1987)

35. After blaming all the usual suspects – the mistakes of the Party, the effects of the era of stagnation, the survivals of the past, the role of enemies of *perestroika* and of 'speculators' in national feelings – the editorial suggested that the original circumstances of the formation of the Soviet Union (*startovye uslovia*), had created a set of structural problems which had still not been overcome. ('Internatsionalistskaya sut' sotsializma', *Kommunist*, no. 13, September 1987, pp. 3–13.)
36. Speech to the Central Committee, 18 February 1988; *Pravda*, 19 February 1988.
37. This phrase echoed earlier explanations of the demonstrations in Alma Ata, as well as of the conflicts over Nagorno-Karabakh, and has become a staple of all current discussions of the sources of inter-ethnic conflict. Whether or not it has any substantial basis in fact, it reflects the difficulty in Soviet discourse of treating national animosities as a potentially autonomous social-psychological phenomenon, and outbursts of conflict or violence as having a spontaneous character. It also reflects a more general disposition toward scapegoating, in which a wide variety of social problems – from shortages of soap to murders of ethnic minorities – are blamed on the manipulations of anti-*perestroika* forces.
38. *Pravda*, 30 July 1988.
39. The text of the resolution was published in *Pravda*, 5 July 1988.
40. In a speech to the Supreme Soviet on 30 May 1989, Gorbachev went even further in his analysis of these distortions:

> In the 1930s Lenin's nationalities policy was subjected to extremely flagrant distortions and deformations . . . An oversimplified understanding of the multifaceted nature of national relations, encouragement of tendencies toward a unitary system, denial of the specific features of national development, political charges against entire nations, with the tyranny and lawlessness stemming therefrom, the impermissible identification of people's national feelings with nationalistic manifestations – all this was part of our life . . . During the time of stagnation, negative processes in national relations were either ignored or driven within, which led to their increasing exacerbation. . . . (*Pravda*, June 1989)

41. *Pravda*, 30 November 1988.
42. Gorbachev's report to the *USSR* Supreme Soviet on 29 November 1988 outlined a three-stage sequence of political reforms. The first stage encompassed the reorganization of national political institutions and the electoral process. Reform of the federal system and of centre–periphery relations would constitute the second stage, and reorganization of local government the third, culminating in the reform of the legal and judicial systems (*Pravda*, 30 November 1988).
43. *Pravda*, 8 January 1989. In his remarks, Gorbachev also went further than ever before in offering assurances of his concern for national values, affirming ' . . . we cannot permit even the smallest people to disappear, the language of even the smallest people to be lost; we cannot permit nihilism with regard to the culture, traditions and history of peoples, be

they big or small. This is what we must state forthrightly at the plenum to be held this summer. And not just state: we shall have to lay down legal foundations and work out an economic and social approach to solving inter-ethnic problems'.

44. *Pravda*, 2 July 1989.
45. *Pravda*, 27 August 1989.
46. Although the platform approved by the Central Committee plenum in 1989 had taken the position that a new treaty was unnecessary, and that the Constitution itself performed that function, Gorbachev subsequently acknowledged that a new framework was needed to restructure centre–republic relations.
47. Address to plenary session of *CPSU* Central Committee, *Pravda*, 9 October 1990, pp. 1–2.

5 New Thinking in Soviet Foreign Policy

Alexander Dallin*

The Gorbachev years have seen a series of fundamental changes in Soviet foreign policy behaviour. They have been accompanied, explicated, and to some extent heralded by equally fundamental changes in Soviet 'thinking' about international affairs.[1]

Especially during the middle years of the Gorbachev era, roughly, 1986–9, the formula, 'New Political Thinking' was widely used by Soviet officials and academics to describe the distinctive approach to international affairs that characterized the Gorbachev cohort. More recently, the use of the term has begun to fade (though Shevardnadze, as Foreign Minister until his sudden resignation in December 1990, continued to use it), but its key elements have by no means been repudiated, and both Soviet conduct and the analysis of world affairs appear to be broadly congruent with the essence of the 'New Political Thinking'.[2]

Its instrumental uses as a Soviet propaganda weapon – first and foremost, to impress others with the novel and benign nature of Gorbachev-era policy – are not of immediate interest to us here, except to note that in general the concept and its content have been successful in helping to transform the image of the Soviet Union abroad; however they have had less than total success in eliciting a symmetrical response – in particular, a conceptual response – from the United States. In any event, this was neither the primary nor the sole purpose of the New Political Thinking.

WHAT IS THE NEW POLITICAL THINKING?

There has never been a precise or authoritative Soviet enumeration of what, for the foreign policy establishment, are the essential elements of the New Political Thinking.[3] None the less, they can be pieced together from Soviet writings and pronouncements. While the term, as it is used in Soviet media, has attributes of publicistic fuzziness, there is in fact a good deal of intellectual coherence and

71

logical consistency to the general approach that is identified by the term and to the more specific propositions and policy implications associated with it.

Whatever its ancestry and paternity – which are controversial – the formulation of new foreign policy thinking, after Gorbachev took over, apparently started from a desire to remove the sense of antagonism that had characterized Soviet relations with the non-communist world. The general orientation of the 'New Thinking' was to normalize the Soviet approach to, and the Soviet role in, the international system. Most concisely, this durable sense of hostility – often accompanied by an assumption of ultimately inevitable conflict – had been reflected in three formulae that were abandoned by the Gorbachev team:

1. The so-called two-camp view, which had divided the world into two hostile camps (corresponding to the underlying doctrinal dichotomy between the forces of progress and reaction);

2. The class approach to international relations, which strove to interpret diplomatic and security relations between nations in Marxist-Leninist terms as a geographic projection of the class struggle (a perspective that had required repeated distortion in explaining world affairs but which was so deeply embedded in Soviet thinking that it proved to be the most difficult concept to abandon);

3. The Leninist formula of *kto kovo*, which in contemporary parlance corresponds to a zero-sum game approach, that is, the assumption that in any relationship one side must ultimately be the total winner, and the other the total loser, rather than allowing (more than tactically) for the recognition and pursuit of shared interests.

Taken together, jettisoning this ballast of orthodox doctrine implied also abandoning the recurrent formula, 'the worse, the better', which had dialectically welcomed a worsening of conditions in the enemy camp as inevitably bringing nearer both objective and subjective conditions for a revolutionary situation.

The postulated hostility between 'world systems' had also contributed to a general policy of autarchy that had isolated the Soviet Union from the international economic system and kept it from fully sharing in world science, technology, and culture – trends that were now recognized to have been costly and wrong.

Abandoning these concepts, the new theorists instead came to view coexistence as a more genuine, enduring, and interactive relationship than had previously been sanctioned. The central thrust was (as David Holloway correctly put it in the title of a recent paper) 'Learning to live and let live'.[4] The key was the novel emphasis on interdependence – in particular, interdependence between Soviet-type and non-Soviet systems – in security affairs as well as in economic and environmental matters. Mutual security – for instance, the novel view that the security of one superpower depended on the perceived security of the other – was illustrative of the new stress on the priority of 'all-human', 'global' (rather than class) interests and values. Such global, non-class issues presumably included the environment, epidemics, and energy, as well as poverty and terrorism.

Implicit in the argument was the search for political rather than military solutions to international problems, and the renunciation of the use of force in the pursuit of political objectives abroad (prompting in turn not only the pursuit of arms control agreements but also a reduction of military budgets and deployments to the level of 'reasonable sufficiency').[5] It also implied a reduction in Soviet expectations in the Third World and in commitments to 'national-liberation' movements there.[6]

WHAT DOES IT AMOUNT TO?

There was a good deal of uncertainty abroad – and some bitter disagreements – over the significance of the rhetoric that was identified with the New Political Thinking. True, over time the initial scepticism (generated in large measure by the repeated disappointment with earlier Soviet overtures) was disspelled as Soviet actions – from Afghanistan to Berlin to Iraq – dramatically bore out the 'unity of theory and practice'.

But even if the notion that the new thinking was a clever trick or purely a public relations operation was largely dismissed, there remained the question whether it was meant merely as a temporary 'breathing-spell' (*peredyshka*), such as had occurred on earlier occasions in Soviet foreign policy, or as a lasting, fundamental change in the Soviet outlook.[7] There was also the question whether it amounted to an ideological *aggiornamento* within the framework of Marxism-Leninism or marked a far-reaching departure from the traditional canons of ideology.[8] Some, in and out of the Soviet

Union, would indeed see the 'New Thinking' as evidence of a betrayal of the faith by the incumbents in the Kremlin.

Meanwhile it became clear – as the New Political Thinking itself has evolved over time – that in its full-blown version it does indeed mark a fundamental departure from the earlier Soviet world view. The general thrust to normalize foreign relations reflects a sense of realism that self-consciously abandons both the utopian goals and the hitherto mandatory ideological scaffolding that has so often distorted Soviet perception. As Eduard Shevardnadze remarked in a revealing comment with regard to Eastern Europe (prior to the autumn of 1989), until now the Soviet Union had sought to remake the people there; now it had concluded that it was easier to remake its policies.

WHAT BROUGHT IT ABOUT?

The New Political Thinking is best seen as the product of several coincident processes. Most obviously, it dramatized the linkage between domestic and foreign policies and perspectives, in this case demonstrating the primacy of domestic over foreign affairs (something Gorbachev and others made quite explicit). Of course, policy decisions have not been the pure product of theoretical ratiocinations, no more than is the case in other countries. Situational factors, at home and abroad, were crucial in triggering the articulation of 'New Thinking' and the implementation of what might be called the new practice.

The major trigger for the formulation of these views was the perception of potentially critical and destabilizing problems within the Soviet Union, beginning with the disastrous state of the economy, and the changing relationship between state and society. Challenges in the Soviet Union's international environment likewise added to the pressures for change. First, all these tension areas showed the Soviet Union to be considerably weaker than had earlier been assumed. Secondly, at a time of stressful domestic transformation the Soviet Union had a strong interest in keeping the international environment as stable, predictable, and benign as possible. And thirdly, under conditions of exceptional tautness in resource allocation, prudence dictated a foreign policy that could produce significantly smaller defence and foreign aid budgets.

The crisis experienced by the Soviet economy and the tensions perceived by Soviet society have remarkably weakened the USSR. In turn, the awareness of that weakness has contributed to the willingness of Soviet circles, official and unofficial, to rethink the ideological bases of Soviet policy. And the unprecedented willingness to admit and deplore the many past misperceptions, miscarriages of justice, mistaken expectations, and misjudgments in domestic priorities and in foreign policy – all these have injected a dose of humility and candour that had been so strikingly absent from Soviet conduct for most of this century. In particular, the policy of *glasnost'* has enabled Soviet writers to deal with topics that had long been taboo. Thus another element was the general atmosphere of *glasnost'*, reformism, and pluralism, in which – as the rest of this book indicates – ideas and orientations that had long been repressed could at last be surfaced and 'New Thinking' was welcomed and encouraged in a variety of fields.

But in addition to these situational factors, the success of the New Thinking was greatly helped by a new generation of Soviet international affairs specialists and diplomats who, during the preceding years, had become acquainted with Western thinking and practice and who had, cautiously and sporadically, begun to integrate the lessons of this experience into their own world view.

In other words, even if the perceived crisis in Soviet policy and society provided an essential trigger for the change of 'thinking', the New Political Thinking was not merely a response to newly-perceived strains and shortages at home.

In this setting a learning process that had quietly been under way for some years could become manifest, particularly as a new generation of actors – officials and academics – acquired access to, or even attained, decision-making levels. Now the New Thinking could be spelled out.

But why should 'mere' words matter to a regime as hard-boiled as that ruling in Moscow? For those reared in the milieu of official Marxism-Leninism, with all the attention paid to careful formulations, and subtle changes in these formulations, and the hazards of deviation from the official course, it was self-evident (as Seweryn Bialer has reiterated) that words mattered greatly; even if, ironically, the very changes taking place marked a fundamental exit from the universe of obligatory doctrinal ritual. The theoretical propositions cited above, and others like them, are important to Soviet foreign policymakers and interpreters. By all indications, they do help to structure the thinking, the perceptions, the analysis of world affairs by Soviet observers and practitioners. (In fact, the West has nothing comparable to offer.) However, they do not – singly or collectively – allow the outsider to predict Soviet foreign policy behaviour with any certainty, even if Moscow chooses to conduct a policy consistent with the New Political Thinking (and of course especially if it need not feel constrained by it).

It is not clear whether the changes in Soviet foreign policy behaviour since 1985 were set in motion before the doctrine was formulated or whether some general structure of 'New Thinking' preceded (or, more likely, accompanied) the changes in policy; it appears that new theoretical formulations were required to legitimize new policy orientations within the Soviet leadership, and in fact significant elements of the New Political Thinking were articulated as early as 1985–6.

Actual Soviet behaviour has in many regards been congruent with this body of thought. Thus the withdrawal from Afghanistan; the decision not to use force in Eastern Europe; the effort to settle regional disputes, from Namibia to Nicaragua to Cambodia; the improvement in relations with China; and the general Soviet–American normalization, including arms control agreements and the realignment with the United States in the Persian Gulf crisis, are all in accord with the new orientation. So is the fresh emphasis on international organizations and Soviet efforts to join new ones, particularly those linked to the promotion of trade and credits.

No doubt not all Soviet foreign policy behaviour has followed from, or vindicated, the New Political Thinking. The unification of Germany was something Moscow had not anticipated and had hoped to avoid. Radical critics in Moscow pointed to Gorbachev's silence over the Tienanmen Square massacre as an example of the regime's hypocrisy. The effort of what had been Union republics, such as the Baltic states, to establish diplomatic and commercial links abroad created unforeseen awkwardness for the Soviet foreign ministry. By and large, however, Shevardnadze's deeds echoed the same orientation as his words.

WHERE DID THE NEW THINKING COME FROM?

There remains the task of tracing the etiology of the New Thinking. It can be shown that many of the ideas advanced since 1985 had been expressed – in more or less public fashion – prior to the Gorbachev era. In this sense the New Political Thinking did not constitute a total hiatus but rather marked the completion, systematization, and publicity of previously adumbrated ideas, and the official endorsement of them, at the expense of other, 'older', political thinking. Thus the priority given to the control and reduction of strategic weapons was not new: some Soviet specialists had keenly perceived the threat of nuclear war and annihilation since the 1950s. The Leninist belief in the inevitability of war had been abandoned a generation before Gorbachev. The two-camp approach, too, had been tacitly dropped back in the Khrushchev era. Disappointment with 'national-liberation movements' in the Third World was voiced by a number of Soviet observers well before 1985. The crystallization of interests shared by the superpowers was not unprecedented.

On the other hand, other elements – most notably, the explicit abandonment of class analysis – were distinctly new; so was the general atmosphere lacking in the traditional animus toward the West and in fact seeking to borrow and copy from it. Above all, views and perspectives that had hitherto been awkwardly interpolated into ritual rhetoric and presented piecemeal in academic circumlocutions, now were made a part of an explicit, reasoned, systematic, and official argument (amounting to a new ideology, some observers abroad would insist, but clearly and importantly one that allowed for far greater flexibility and pragmatism).

POLITICS AND PUBLIC OPINION

Within the Soviet Union, the New Political Thinking has not been unanimously or wholeheartedly accepted by the attentive public, although it wrought considerably less havoc than some of the 'New Thinking' on economic affairs. Some officials have had difficulty in jettisoning the 'old thinking'; for instance, seeing the world in Manichean terms of 'us' and 'them' has been second nature to many. Others have emphatically disagreed with significant parts of the new 'thinking', such as its Western (and Westernizing) orientation. In most instances, we find a close linkage between foreign and domestic policy preferences of particular actors: an individual's willingness to accept and assimilate the principles of the New Thinking correlates positively with his or her favourable orientation toward the general reform outlook of the Gorbachev era (such as *glasnost'* and the establishment of a law-governed state), but there are exceptions to this rule.

The new body of ideas and its consequences are part of the skein that the orthodox die-hards in the Soviet Communist Party have attacked – at first, mostly behind the scenes or by indirection, and then, openly, as Soviet politics polarized. In particular, former Politburo member Yegor Ligachev voiced his dissent from the priority of all-human over class interests: 'We proceed from the class nature of international relations. Any other formulation of the issue only introduces confusion into the thinking of Soviet people and our friends abroad. . ..'[9] Quite logically, in 1990, Ligachev and his political allies accused the reformists of having surrendered Eastern Europe, having permitted the strengthening of Japan and the reunification of Germany, having cut the defence budget, and having contributed to the disintegration of the Soviet state.[10] If the Soviet Union loomed less formidable in 1990 than it had in 1980 or 1970, this was blamed on the outlook of the Gorbachev team.

It would be fairer to suggest that the change in perceptions reflected an unpublicized shift of values and priorities: the reformist leaders (like Eduard Shevardnadze and Aleksandr Yakovlev) by implication did not believe that the continuation of the war in Afghanistan or the forcible suppression of dissent in Eastern Europe was worth the price; in reactions in the West, in resources committed, in other opportunities and benefits foregone, and in political costs at home.

But this was no longer an esoteric debate among the few insiders. One consequence of the political changes in the Soviet Union has been the replacement of the traditional façade of monolithic unanimity by the celebration of pluralism of opinions, which now extends to foreign affairs as well (though somewhat less than on domestic matters). Another consequence has been the mushrooming of public opinion research, conducted with varying but increasing sophistication and reliability.

One study of particular relevance to our topic was that directed by Andrei Melville and Alexander Nikitin (both then with the Institute for the Study of the USA and Canada in Moscow) in cooperation with Brown University. The results of a survey of 120 international affairs specialists, scholars, journalists, and diplomats were published in 1989.[11] A second phase was conducted in Moscow and Kursk with a sample of 1200 persons representing (or intended to represent) all strata of Soviet (urban) society.

The data shows broad support for the priority of 'all-human' interests and values, ahead of state, class, or other narrower interests.[12] Almost 80 per cent disagreed with the statement that the principal aim of Soviet foreign policy must be to assist the spread of socialism as a system on a world scale. Some 77 per cent believed that the prevention of nuclear war should be the principal aim of Soviet foreign policy, ranked ahead of any 'class' purposes. When the interviewers structured a hypothetical conflict between the interests of proletarian internationalism and all-human interests, only 9 per cent of the respondents felt that internationalist help to progressive forces abroad must have the top priority. 71 per cent of the citizens and 87 per cent of the specialists gave, in such a conflict situation, priority to all-human values and interests.

In terms of the assimilation of the substance of the 'New Political Thinking', the available data suggests the existence of some six distinct groups within the Soviet 'attentive public'. This typology is based both on a reading of the Soviet press (general and specialized alike) and on a series of interviews conducted by this writer in Moscow in the spring of 1990.

1. There are the real, convinced 'new thinkers', both the creative ones and others who have sincerely internalized the concepts. A number of academics as well as practitioners belong here. While they may differ among themselves, these tend to be people who are, firstly, relatively 'unideological' in their belief systems, that is, un-dogmatic, flexible, and capable of learning; and, secondly, relatively comfortable in Western political and social science environments. Some of them stumbled upon elements of the 'New Thinking' by acquaintance with the outside world in the 1960s and 1970s. Most of them came out of the official Soviet/CPSU milieu but had become disappointed or even alienated prior to 1985. An important part of this group is probably made up of those who cut their political teeth in the Khrushchev days (the group of 'consultants' like Fedor Bur-latsky, Oleg Bogomolov, and Aleksandr Bovin are a good example), but increasingly this type is also represented by the next younger group.

2. A different category seems to consist of people who are typi-cally compliant converts to the New Thinking but have difficulty fully letting go of earlier beliefs. Some, for instance, have difficulty jetti-soning a basically dichotomic view of the world even if they eagerly identify with the new Soviet–American connection. The class struggle is something else they have difficulty letting go of in foreign

affairs. And yet they eagerly embrace 'global issues', even if they are unsure what to do with them. Some people in this group may have sincere difficulty in squaring the New Thinking with an equally sincere Russian patriotism. There are some such people in the Ministry of Foreign Affairs and elsewhere in the government and Party.

3. Then there is the category of obedient, though sometimes sullen and reluctant, members of the establishment who mouth the tenets of the New Thinking indifferently, without particular conviction, just as they pronounced the false verities of earlier days with an equal lack of conviction and with an equal show of dedication (or self-interest). Without always being clear about this in their own minds, they may assume that the New Thinking is an instrumental, temporary business, to be succeeded some day by another phase of Soviet foreign policy concepts, and the whole trick is to remain alert, responsive, and loyal to the authorities, quick to learn the arguments that make any given phase – new thinking included – indisputable truths in their time. This group includes a good many people who for many years shone in their anti-American dedication and have difficulty fully shedding it now; it also includes some who worked with or on the East European 'fraternal' parties and states and have difficulty accepting their abandonment and disappearance.

4. Harder to pin down is the group of 'old thinkers' who are now trying to hide their beliefs. The 'New Thinking' turns out to be particularly difficult to swallow for those who have professionally been committed to work that is now downgraded (for example, people in some of the departments and institutes attached to the Central Committee). Typically, along with a rhetorical acceptance of the New Thinking, for instance, as an instrumental device to increase the Soviet appeal abroad, there is continued stress on the contradictions and conflicts within the capitalist world and on the bright future of socialism. In fact, some of them are not aware of continuing to mouth some of the 'old' rhetoric.

5. And then there are the 'real old thinkers' who remain prepared to put across their orthodox views in so far as they find it politic or safe in the present environment. The classic case may well be Yegor Ligachev's strictures, cited earlier (1988), and his charges that the Gorbachev policy has strengthened the hand of the imperialists (1990). The reactions at the Founding Congress of the Russian Com-

munist Party in June 1990 suggest that among die-hards and true believers there is some sympathy for this view of the New Political Thinking as a betrayal of the faith. Some Soviet military figures have made clear that they likewise have reservations – generally, not so much the 'thinking' as its practical pay-off, such as unilateral arms reductions, the 'surrender' of Eastern Europe, a new defensive doctrine, and a lowering of defence expenditures. Similarly, there are those who charge the leadership with abandoning comrades and clients abroad.

Speaking up on foreign and defence policy issues at a party congress is virtually unprecedented in the memory of the present generation and must be seen primarily, not as an effort to change foreign policy thinking or behaviour, but as part of drawing up a comprehensive indictment of the Gorbachev regime.

6. As of 1990–1, it is necessary to propose one more opinion group that is only beginning to take shape – those on the radical end of the Soviet political spectrum for whom the Gorbachev team is too hesitant, too compromising, or too rigid.[13] These are observers inclined to stress the frequent divergence of Soviet practice from professed principles, be it on dealings with China after Tienanmen Square, or Soviet aid to North Korea or Cuba. They are also likely to press for a greater role in foreign affairs for the Supreme Soviet, for political parties, and for the Union republics.

All in all, with all the ups and downs in public support, the foreign policy of the Gorbachev regime and the 'thinking' undergirding it appear to have been accepted with varying degrees of conviction and intensity but also with relatively little dissent from either left or right. But in large part the verdict on the acceptance of the New Political Thinking remains open in so far as it is largely derivative of other, broader, political developments at home and abroad.

WHO DONE IT?

Three groups appear to have had a special role in the formation and acceptance of the New Political Thinking. First of all, it benefited substantially from the emergence on the political arena of a new generation – both practitioners and academics, mostly in their thirties and forties – who have had the opportunity to serve or travel abroad and have not only broader general education and better linguistic skills, but also familiarity with Western writings in the social sciences and international relations, as well as different methodologies of research and styles of argument and debate.

While this cohort included some older officials with diplomatic experience in the United States or at the United Nations (such as Vladimir Petrovsky) and some 'fast learners' without the benefit of such service (including Eduard Shevardnadze), the bulk of 'New Thinking' came in the form of memoranda and briefings from younger men (mostly in academic institutes, in the foreign service, or in journalism) whose skills, polish, and mode of thinking for the first time rivalled those of their Western counterparts, who for many of them did indeed serve as an explicit or implicit reference group. Increasingly accompanied by a sense of shame and frustration caused by the perceived backwardness of their own country and expressions of anger about the sacrifice of generations to a tissue of fictions and falsehoods, these were important cadres for the fresh approach.

For the moment it remains a hypothesis that their collective role was decisive in effectively putting forward – in conversations, in drafts of official documents, and in memoranda to their superiors – many of the ideas that came to be identified with the New Political Thinking.[14]

Secondly, a more senior group close to the new leadership advised the decision-makers in the same vein. This group includes political scientists who were all products of the Khrushchev era, like Georgii Shakhnazarov (later, personal adviser to Gorbachev), Yevgeniy Primakov (later, a candidate member of the Politburo and subsequently a member of Gorbachev's Presidential Council) and Fedor Burlatsky (later, editor of *Literaturnaya gazeta*).

And thirdly, some key policymakers (notably, Eduard Shevardnadze and Aleksandr Yakovlev) had to be prepared to listen and accept new formulae and approaches. The coincidence of these three groups (and the smaller number of actors at the core of foreign policy decision-making) made the appearance of the 'New Thinking' in foreign policy relatively smooth and simple, compared to the more bitterly contested issue areas like economic reform or the future of the Communist Party. Moreover, the later complaints of hardliners like Ligachev that they had been by-passed in the formulation of new foreign policy principles (complaints that ring true) suggest that Shevardnadze was able to keep the official formulation of the New Political Thinking away from those whom he had reason to suspect of hostility to it.

CONCLUSION

The New Political Thinking, it has become apparent, is itself not a constant. Under conditions when there is no longer a 'general line' dispensed by the ruling party, and when individual scholars and publicists can give alternative views and versions of such a body of doctrine, it is both natural, healthy, and disconcerting that its operational meaning remains somewhat elusive and fluid. Soviet 'round-tables', published in prestigious political journals, recognize that Soviet thinking is full of unanswered questions – especially because standard 'socialist' beliefs are not explicitly cast out but rather remain in ambiguous coexistence with the new world-order notions.

And yet, while it may thus suffer as a body of abstract ideas, and while its fate may thus be tied to what happens in Soviet politics writ large, the 'New Thinking' has signalled a profound change of values and attitudes precisely where the 'old thinking' had been most troubling to the outside world. Whatever happens in Moscow, much of the 'New Thinking' is virtually certain to remain valid for future foreign policymakers and analysts there.

Notes

*I am most grateful to the Rockefeller Foundation for the opportunity to draft this paper at its Study and Conference Center at Bellagio, Italy. Research for this chapter was supported in part by a grant from the International Research and Exchanges Board, with funds provided by the National Endowment for the Humanities and the U.S. Information Agency. None of these organizations is responsible for the views expressed here.

1. There is by now a considerable literature on the 'New Political Thinking' in foreign and security affairs. One continuing controversy among Western observers has concerned the level, or the depth, of changes – whether what has changed is rhetoric, doctrine, ideology, theory, or thought. See, for example, Vendulka Kubalkova and A. A. Cruickshank, *Thinking About Soviet 'New Thinking'* (Berkeley, CA.: Institute of International Studies, 1989) and sources cited therein; Seweryn Bialer, '"New Thinking" and Soviet Foreign Policy', *Survival*, July–August 1988, pp. 291–309; Robert Legvold, 'The Revolution in Soviet Foreign Policy', *Foreign Affairs: America and the World*, 1988–9, pp. 82–98; Allen Lynch, 'The Continuing Importance of Ideology in Soviet Foreign Policy', in *Harriman Institute Forum*, 3:7 (July 1990); Margot Light, *The Soviet Theory of International Relations* (Brighton, Sussex:

Wheatsheaf Books, 1988), chapter 10; Cynthia Roberts and Elizabeth Wishnick, 'Ideology is Dead! Long Live Ideology!', *Problems of Communism*, November–December 1989, pp. 57–69; and Sylvia Woodby, *Gorbachev and the Decline of Ideology in Soviet Foreign Policy* (Boulder: Westview Press, 1989). In addition see *How Should America Respond to Gorbachev's Challenge? A Report of the Task Force on Soviet New Thinking* (New York: Institute for East–West Security Studies, 1987). In my view what matters most is the nature and the substance of the change, rather than definitional squabbles. See also notes 7 and 8 below.

2. There are several possible explanations as to why its use has been on the decline. Critics have at times blamed the New Political Thinking for unwelcome consequences (such as the reunification of Germany). Perhaps, in the face of a rather chaotic reality, the leadership has moderated its efforts to portray the changes in Soviet conduct as the carefully thought-out products of 'New Thinking'. Moreover, it is now recognized that the diversity of views bracketed by the 'New Thinking' has left a number of 'contradictions' unresolved.

3. Different Western writers have come up with different enumerations of what they consider the essential elements of the New Political Thinking, the number varying from three to ten. There is no 'right' or 'wrong' number. See, for example, Kubalkova and Cruickshank, *Thinking About Soviet 'New Thinking'* (Berkeley, CA.: Institute of International Studies, 1989); Boris Meissner, '"New Thinking" and Soviet Foreign Policy', *Aussenpolitik* (English edn), no. 2, 1989, pp. 101–18; David Holloway, 'Gorbachev's "New Thinking"', *Foreign Affairs: America and the World*, 1988–9, pp. 66–81.

4. David Holloway, 'Learning to Live and Let Live', in Abraham Brumberg (ed.), *Chronicle of a Revolution* (New York: Pantheon, 1990), pp. 145–160.

5. For discussions of 'New Thinking' in security matters, see, for example, Tsuyoshi Hasegawa, 'Gorbachev, The New Thinking of Foreign-Security Policy and the Military', in Peter Juviler and Hiroshi Kimura (eds), *Gorbachev's Reforms* (New York: Aldine de Gruyter, 1988), pp. 115–147; Stephen Meyer, 'The Sources and Prospects of Gorbachev's New Political Thinking on Security', *International Security*, 13:2 (1988), pp. 124–163; Stephen Shenfield, *The Nuclear Predicament* (London: Chatham House Papers, no. 37, 1987); Matthew Evangelista, 'The New Soviet Approach to Security', *World Policy Journal*, Autumn 1986, pp. 561–99; Bruce Parrott, 'Soviet National Security Under Gorbachev', *Problems of Communism*, November–December 1988, pp. 1–36; and Raymond Garthoff, *Deterrence and the Revolution in Soviet Military Doctrine* (Washington, DC: Brookings, 1990). See also Richard Smoke and Andrei Kortunov (eds), *Mutual Security: A New Approach* (New York: St. Martin's, 1990). On the implications of the 'New Thinking' for the Soviet view of international law (including the Soviet position on international arbitration), see William E. Butler (ed.), *Perestroika and International Law* (Dordrecht: Martinus Nijhoff, 1990).

6. Soviet writings on the Third World have been amply and ably analyzed in

the publications of, among others, David Albright, Francis Fukuyama, Jerry Hough and Elizabeth Valkenier. See also Galia Golan, *Gorbachev's 'New Thinking' on Terrorism* (Washington Papers, no. 141, New York: Praeger, 1990).

7. For examples of the sceptics, see Gerhard Wettig, 'Gorbachev and "New Thinking" in the Kremlin's Foreign Policy', *Aussenpolitik* (English edn), no. 2, 1987, pp. 144–54; William Odom, 'How Far Can Soviet Reform Go?', *Problems of Communism*, vol. 36 (November–December 1987), no. 6; and Stephen Sestanovich, 'Gorbachev's Foreign Policy: A Diplomacy of Decline', *Problems of Communism*, vol. 37 (January–February 1988), no. 1.

8. Kubalkova and Cruickshank represented the most sophisticated but ultimately erroneous view that the New Political Thinking was but 'an attempt by the Soviet superpower to find a Marxist foreign policy foundation that is not only significantly different from that of the United States, but also will allow the socio-economically weaker USSR to establish the rules and set the pace in the next phase of the "historical struggle"' between the two systems (Kubalkova and Cruickshank, *Thinking About Soviet 'New Thinking'* (Berkeley, CA.: Institute of International Studies, 1989) p. 114). They pointed, rather prematurely, to Eastern Europe, anti-Americanism, and strategic doctrine as three areas in which the New Political Thinking has not brought about any change.

9. *Pravda*, 6 August 1988.

10. See, for example, *Pravda*, 26 June, 5 and 11 July 1990; *International Herald Tribune*, 27 June 1990.

11. *SShA*, no. 9, 1989.

12. A. Yu. Mel'vil' and A. I. Nikitin, 'Konets "yedinomysliia"? Sovetskoe obshchestvennoe mnenie po voprosam bezopasnosti i mezhdunarodnykh otnoshenii' (typescript, 1990).

13. See, for example, A. Kortunov and A. Izyumov, 'Chto ponimat' pod gosudarstvennymi interesami vo vneshnei politike', *Literaturnaya gazeta*, no. 28, 1990; 'Novoe myshlenie v mezhdunarodnykh delakh', *Kommunist* (Moscow), no. 8, 1989, pp. 98–107; Suzanne Crow, 'Moscow Looks Hard at Its Foreign Aid Programme' (Radio Liberty), *Report on the USSR*, 2:32 (10 August 1990), pp. 8–9.

14. On the role of the *institutchiki*, see, for example, Scott R. Atkinson, *Soviet Defense Policy Under Gorbachev: The Growing Civilian Influence* (Alexandria, VA: Center for Naval Analyses, Occasional Paper, March 1990).

6 New Thinking about World Communism

Alexander Dallin*

A good deal has been said and written about the relevance of the 'New Political Thinking' to Soviet foreign and security policy – the subjects of arms control, Soviet–American relations and regional problems have been much discussed. We have heard much less about the attitude of the Gorbachev regime – or popular attitudes – toward international communism, the Soviet bloc, and the prospect of 'world revolution'.

There are three major reasons for this relative neglect on the Soviet side. One is the recognition that world revolution is a most unpromising avenue for the Soviet Union to pursue or bank on, particularly at a time when attention is focused on more exciting and more urgent topics. A second reason is the fact that the 'New Thinking' and current policy are largely in the hands of diplomats, international relations and international security specialists who have had little time for and little interest in international communism and for many of whom it has long been an esoteric and 'ideological' topic of little or no relevance to 'real' international affairs. And thirdly, in so far as the official articulation of the New Thinking was, for some years, circumscribed by domestic political tactics, it had appeared wise not to advertise the provocative departure from orthodox verities in an area where the ideologues were apt to respond with particular sensitivity and venom, for here the revisionism was bound to touch on some fundamentals of Marxism-Leninism.

By 1990 that latter effort had proved pointless. The bitter differences within the Soviet establishment were out in the open. But this was the culmination of a process that had taken time. The move toward greater candour and insight has been gradually gaining momentum since 1985. At that time old-style Soviet hardliners like Oleg Rakhmanin (writing under the pseudonyms Borisov and Vladimirov[1]) were, if anything, tightening the net of legitimate diversity, warning of revisionism and nationalism among communists in the face of what they claimed was an unprecedented onslaught by the imperialists.[2]

While the reformists in the saddle had other priorities, by 1987 senior independent publicists like Aleksandr Bovin were taking advantage of the new *glasnost'* to write derisively of the customary communist attempts to depict the course of events – whatever the course, whatever the events – as being in harmony with the predicted unfolding of the inevitable. History, he wrote, 'mocks attempts to control its course'. Thus, it had to be admitted that the prospects of socialist revolution were not at all what had been expected. Bovin argued:

> Above all, it should be acknowledged that the ability of capitalism to adapt to the new historical setting has surpassed our expectations. The prospect of socialist transformations in developed capitalist countries has receded indefinitely.

As for the Third World,

> In a number of countries of socialist orientation, the situation remains unstable, fraught with the possibility of regression.

More generally,

> Both in capitalist countries and in Third World countries, the communist parties, with few exceptions, have failed to become mass organizations, to win for themselves the support of the bulk of the working class, of the toilers.

One of the reasons for these failures had been the failure of the Soviet Union and other socialist countries to provide an attractive model.

> The society that, by all indications, should have been an example, a model to be imitated, a stimulus in the struggle for the socialist reordering of society, has not been created in the Soviet Union.

The same had been true of China as well. Here, too, the equivalent of a *perestroika*, Bovin argued, at least held out a hope for the future.[3]

Such articles set out many of the themes that were to be developed in the following years. Typically the journalists spoke out first. After them came the diplomats and other practitioners, then the scholars, and finally the ideologues. In March 1988, the journal *MEMO* (*Mirovaya ekonomika i mezhdunarodnye otnosheniia*) published a major article by its editor, German Diligensky, which went a good deal further and deeper in questioning traditional assumptions concerning revolutions abroad, but still from a Leninist perspective.[4] By early 1990 a Communist Party journal could devote a remarkably candid roundtable to the same subject.[5]

THEMES AND ARGUMENTS

While they tended to become more radical and outspoken over time, most such analyses could be fitted into the same general framework. They tried to provide answers to three questions: 1. In what ways have we (or our predecessors) been wrong about the prospects of revolution (whose inevitability and ultimate success Marxists had been taking for granted)?   2. What are the sources of our errors?   3. What follows from this realization?

There was little argument about the first proposition. In the major capitalist countries – indeed, the most highly developed ones – such as the United States, Britain, and Germany, the communist parties were a pitiful joke; in France and even Italy, where they had a mass following, they were losing support. In the Third World, countries of allegedly socialist orientation were turning elsewhere instead. Well before the crisis in Eastern Europe in the autumn of 1989, Moscow recognized that even within the 'socialist commonwealth' there were serious problems that required study and reform. But in regard to the second and third points above opinions varied. Moreover, while the gloves were off, for some time there remained the prudential convention that no one turned overtly against the very idea of a socialist revolution (although its essence and meaning could be, and were, widely, questioned, and it no longer needed to be equated with 'proletarian' revolution or indeed any violent revolution at all).

The search for the sources of erroneous past (and present) analyses led the writers into the labyrinth of Marxism-Leninism.[6] This reopened the linked issues of the nature of capitalism, the socialist model, and the future of the Third World. It was no longer a matter of ritual or dogma that the infallibility of the 'classics' of Marxism-Leninism needed unquestioningly to be reaffirmed. Soviet writers now condemned the 'stereotype of bipolarity' – socialism and capitalism as the only alternatives – that was the product of vulgar

Marxism. Others questioned the 'myth' of the victorious 'historical mission of the working class'. Now it could be acknowledged that for decades the class struggle and class antagonisms had been 'absolutized' by communist analysts and mechanically given undue importance. Historians were arguing against the previously mandatory stress on *zakonomernost'* – the insistence that history proceeded in conformity with immutable laws of social development – and instead pleaded for *al'ternativnost'* – room for choices and alternative paths.

It turned out that nationalization did not in itself give workers a sense of ownership and identification with their enterprise. Another axiom that was likewise challenged concerned the equation of the interests of the international proletariat and those of the Soviet Union.

> We are being greatly harmed [declared a professor at the Central Committee's training school for foreign communists] when we try to strengthen our [international] position by referring to the fact that we, as it were automatically, represent the interests of the entire international proletariat – all 670 million people. That is simply incorrect. The scope and the diversity of the interests of the working class cannot be represented by any one party or movement. . ... One must not automatically arrogate to oneself the ability to represent all the aspirations of the international working class, especially those beyond the borders of our country.[7]

Soviet publications convey, to a greater degree than personal interviews do, an instrumental, utilitarian approach: to what extent must the old ideological baggage be jettisoned in order to rescue the essence of the cause? At least in print authors – especially those in official Soviet positions – will reaffirm that, in spite of all, the class struggle is not just fading away; that the working class remains essential as the architect of historical change; that sooner or later it must pass from defence to offence; that since current conditions favour evolution rather than revolution and 'global' rather than 'class' objectives, international communism must stress working together with others, such as social-democrats and 'greens'.

Others, however, will much more candidly admit the bankruptcy of communist thinking. After the many years of glossing over all unpleasantness and the repetition of abstractions and stereotypes removed from real life, it is not too much to speak of 'pessimism, disappointment, and disorientation' among communist analysts, of a 'crisis' in world communism (words used in recent Soviet publications on the subject). While a few commentators (like Aleksandr Tsipko) will dismiss Marxism altogether for its utopias and myths that they hold responsible for the distortions of the Soviet era, a greater number find it convenient to stress the changes that have intervened since Marx's or Lenin's days. Thus, the working class was no longer what it had been. On the one hand, it was argued, it had become more conscious, more sophisticated, more 'civilized', more inclined to favour gradualism and to reject violence in favour of 'parliamentary, peaceful, and democratic' forms of struggle. Labour had become less emotional and more rational in its political attitudes, it was argued; indeed, it tended to be suspicious of all -isms. (In fact, large segments of the workforce in developed and developing societies were on the far right, politically. How could this be explained?)

On the other hand, the working class in the West (and that is where most of the attention of Soviet analysts was) had undergone important structural changes – and here different Soviet analysts had their own explanations – be it the inclusion of 'scientific workers' and the vast expansion of white-collar workers or the qualitative stratification within the working class(es). Some analysts found it hard to say what interests all types of labour had in common that distinguished them from all other strata of society.

At the same time, capitalism was no longer the brutal exploiter. Soviet observers, it was commonly agreed, had underestimated the vitality of Western capitalism and the ability of the state to introduce reforms that seemingly went against the interests of the ruling class. The areas of alienation and exploitation had been reduced, and so consequently had the workers' hostility to the system. The government had typically imposed elements of social responsibility, welfare, and security that mitigated the potential effects of economic crises. Moreover, internationalization of production and international cooperation among capitalist states rendered the old images of intracapitalist conflict obsolete. (Soviet authors have been more reluctant to tinker with the Leninist notion of imperialism, but some – including Bovin – have cast it overboard, if only, they argue, because imperialism has changed fundamentally since Lenin's days.)

There was some implicit disagreement over the question whether or not the changes had an 'objective' basis that could somehow be integrated into a Marxist perspective. Some commentators attributed the change in the working class primarily to the 'scientific-technological revolution' that had recently intervened. Others associated the priority of global values with the advent of nuclear weapons.

More cruel critics, by contrast, candidly stressed the basic error of communist categories and axioms. One result, once this was recognized (a historian suggested) was that communists now had no answers other than reformism, that is, they now found themselves groping for political space already occupied by others. The working class in advanced societies, another argued, had changed qualitatively, including its culture and values and had no use for communists as they had come to know them in the past. Others argued that the root of the problem was more basic: to begin with the error was the Marxists' assumptions. A. I. Volkov, a historian, declared at a roundtable on this subject:

A realistic assessment of contemporary capitalism, its development, its vitality, is in fundamental conflict with the assumptions of communists – so to speak, with our genetic code, which consists of the notion that human happiness can be achieved only by means of revolution, which is understood as the forcible redistribution of property and power. This is an illusion, since hopes can be tied not to redistribution but only to some higher form of production. Today's developed societies have demonstrated the possibility, in principle, to solve social problems far more painlessly and more effectively, permitting these societies to rise to a higher level of development not by means of destruction but by building and assimilating the best of the achievements of earlier generations and forms of organization of social life. . ..[8]

One old-timer declared that international communism had always lagged behind the times. It had lagged in recognizing that capitalism had recovered in the 1920s, it had lagged in identifying fascism as enemy number one, it had lagged in identifying the national-liberation movements as a promising ally, it had erroneously attacked Eurocommunism as anti-Leninist, and so forth: all in all, what was called for was a 'reconsideration of many ideological positions of the communist movement'. In 1917–19, another observer remarked that the worldwide victory of socialism was expected in months. 'Then months turned into years, and years into decades. The current vision of the emergence of socialism measures this process in hundreds of years'.[9]

One historian was mindful of the prominence world revolution had

had in the early days of the Soviet regime, as Lenin himself had acknowledged. Arriving at the Finland Station, Lenin had proclaimed, 'Long live the world socialist revolution!' The 1924 Constitution of the USSR provided for the inclusion of all future Soviet republics in the Soviet Union, the final goal being the 'uniting of the toilers of all countries in the World Socialist Soviet Republic'. It was true that, Stalin, in his interview with Roy Howard (1 March 1936), had hypocritically denied that there had been such a goal: 'We never had such plans or intentions. . .. This is the fruit of . . . tragicomical misunderstanding'. All the more reason now to get the story straight.

TYPES OF RESPONSES

While the positions of different commentators are still in flux, and some public statements may not represent their actual views fairly, one may suggest an emerging typology of responses to the shared recognition of a crisis in the 'international labour movement' or, more properly, in the communist world. In simplest terms, they divide into those who believe one of the following propositions:

1. In all essential respects Marx and Lenin were right and their theories remain largely valid, though their application has at times been faulty.

2. Marxism-Leninism was correct in its day, but the world has changed in significant ways, which require a fresh look and a new political orientation. Thus, instead of appealing to the working class, communists should now appeal to the entire society. Though Lenin attacked social-chauvinism and social-opportunism, this must not mean the rejection of reformism for all times. Similarly, a fresh look is in order with regard to the Third World (a topic on which Soviet observers divide and which by its complexity exceeds the bounds of this chapter, but on which Soviet observers increasingly acknowledge their disappointment and a recognition that developments in even 'progressive' societies have scarcely lived up to Soviet expectations).

3. In a number of fundamental respects, Marxism-Leninism turns out always to have been in error. Serious doubts are in order about the whole notion of historical inevitability. Marxism is deficient in

lacking moral categories. It is impossible effectively to direct a world movement from a single centre, just as it is impossible for Gosplan effectively to direct the entire Soviet economy. Or putting it more gently, there were in Marxism serious contradictions that needed to be highlighted, exposed, and amended, though they did not require abandoning socialism *in toto*.[10]

4. Never mind the theory, which can always be manipulated; what is needed is new guidance to practice – for example, an appeal to the Socialist International to work together (that is, neither to ostracize it nor to merge with it). The narrowest, most utilitarian approach is to argue that since communists abroad were doing so poorly, what was needed was a broad coalition of social forces (read: political parties and movements).

5. International communism has been a vast failure – misleading and expensive at that – and it will be wise for the Soviet authorities to disengage from it as undramatically and as elegantly as possible, writing it off as the product of an earlier era.

All in all, world communism and world revolution have receded, in the minds of most Soviet observers and policymakers, to a distant, dubious, and dependent role – compared to urgent and immediate needs, compared to domestic priorities, and compared to international security, economics, and diplomatic tasks, in a general atmosphere of 'de-ideologization'.[11] In all these regards, the place assigned to world communism and world revolution in the context of the New Political Thinking represents the logical though important next step in a process of evolution that began with the first doubts soon after the October Revolution. Not so the dominant reaction to events in the 'socialist camp'.

THE SOCIALIST CAMP

Curiously, the 'New Political Thinking' – focusing first and foremost on Soviet–American relations – had little to say about Soviet relations with 'socialist countries'. True, Mikhail Gorbachev in his UN General Assembly speech in December 1988 stressed freedom of choice for all countries – presumably, including allegiance and development path. In November 1986 he had distributed to his colleagues a memorandum, discussed at a working meeting of the leaders of ruling communist parties in Moscow, which dealt with equalizing relations among the 'fraternal countries'. Gradually a sense developed that the tolerance of diversity – pluralism – within the Soviet Union also applied to relations within the socialist camp (provided that diversity was limited to 'socialist' systems and did not jeopardize security relations).[12]

A large part of the Soviet elite perceived that there were troubling aspects to Soviet relations with Eastern Europe; the Polish events of 1980–1 had caused particular concern. But the general feeling, in the 1980s, was that the East European governments had gained, or were gaining, legitimacy at home; that there was no crisis at hand; and that problematic issues (such as the Nazi–Soviet deal of 1939, or Soviet responsibility for the Katyn massacre) were finally being addressed. In the words of a leading Soviet party official:

> The elements of 'paternalistic' relations, in which we, as it were, played the role of patron, are gone. The need for strictly observing the equality principle, which was advanced before, has been reaffirmed in the spirit of New Thinking by the conclusion that no party has a monopoly on the truth of socialism, and only the strengthening of socialism in practice can serve as criteria of this truth. It is no longer viewed as harmful to the unity of socialist countries that there exist different ideas of how to build a new society and that individual socialist countries may have their specific national and state interests. In light of New Thinking we have fully realized that the most reliable way to unity lies not in the mechanical unification of these countries, but in the persistent search for solutions based on a balance of their interests, and our common socialist foundation provides the most favourable conditions for this.[13]

True, 'it is obvious that the increasing democratization of mutual relations brings out more clearly than before the existence of certain contradictions between socialist countries because at times their national interests do not coincide on some specific issues'. In fact, 'an analysis of the situation indicates that cooperation with our friends has not yet reached a true turning point'.[14] A few months later Vitali Zhurkin, Director of the Europe Institute at the USSR Academy of Sciences, could recall:

. . . some time in the past we arrived at a consensus on the inevitability of reform in Eastern Europe. But we all believed quite sincerely that they would take ten to fifteen years and would come about gently, advancing at a leisurely pace. Yet what happened was explosions . . . .[15]

In 1989 Soviet officials, from Gorbachev on down, had made public declarations that what in the West was called the 'Brezhnev Doctrine' was no longer in force. While this was a bit of a charade (if only because there never had been a Brezhnev Doctrine), it was none the less significant in marking the Soviet renunciation of the use of force in regard to Eastern Europe – and was so understood.[16]

By all indications, the sequence of events in Eastern Europe that led to the ouster or replacement of governments from East Berlin to Bucharest surprised the masters in Moscow as much as it did observers in the West – and this, in spite of the fact that it was Soviet signals that were crucial in triggering the whole chain of events. What is of particular interest in the context of this chapter is the conceptual response. The reformist wing in Moscow did not hesitate to express their approval. What took place in Eastern Europe, wrote Vladimir Lukin, a prominent foreign affairs specialist and more recently Chairman of the International Relations Committee of the RSFSR Supreme Soviet, was 'the result of a series of sweeping antitotalitarian democratic revolutions'.

The Soviet Union's reaction to the events in Eastern Europe has been most reassuring. We seem to be learning – better late than never – to tell the interests of genuine national security from a desire to keep 'our people' in power in neighbouring European capitals.[17]

It was true that events in Eastern Europe went further than even Soviet reformers would have wished, but consistent commentators dismissed this as within the range of the tolerable: once Moscow had agreed not to intervene, the consequences had to be worked out without an active Soviet role. For some people, another commentator explained, the events in Eastern Europe were a cause for euphoria; for others they were a source of pain and bitterness. 'To my mind, what happened had to happen. A positive process is taking place, mirroring a world-wide tendency. Its essence is the transition from totalitarianism to parliamentary pluralism, civil society, and a state of law'.[18]

And yet, a good many members of the Soviet foreign affairs community seemed to have lost their power of speech. No doubt it was a serious ideological and political embarrassment to be obliged to acknowledge that the inevitable course of history had been reversed and communist governments were forced from office, from the Baltic to the Black Sea. Indeed, it took some months for serious theoretical treatments of the events to appear; Soviet journals acknowledge that 'regrettably, no coherent conceptual analysis' of the events has as yet been offered.

But the bitterness ran deep. After being variously hinted at for months, an overt attack on the policy – and the outlook – that had brought about the collapse of the East European bloc, and with it, of the Warsaw Pact, came in June 1990 from the same quarters who had attacked other elements of the New Political Thinking and now found a responsive audience at the Founding Congress of the Russian Communist Party; it was repeated at the Twenty-Eighth Party Congress the following month. Yegor Ligachev charged the new thinkers – presumably including Gorbachev and certainly including Shevardnadze – with selling out the comrades and betraying the principles of communist solidarity. General Albert Makashov dwelt on the security implications of the set-back. Both voiced alarm at the prospect of a formidable new united Germany that the Soviet people had fought so hard to defeat. If this was the result of the New Thinking, it was a danger to the health of the Soviet Union (as was, the hardliners argued, Gorbachev's policy toward the Soviet nationalities).[19] Curiously, most of the arguments – on both sides – were couched in terms of national security and patriotism, not in the traditional jargon or rhetoric of 'proletarian internationalism'.

Perhaps the most powerful reply to the various charges came from Shevardnadze, who likened the innuendo of Soviet criticism to Senator Joseph McCarthy's campaign in the United States that had asked, forty years earlier, 'Who lost China?'

> Strange as it may seem, recently we too have had similar accusations. One gets the impression that some people would love to conduct an investigation on 'Who lost Eastern Europe?' Some people seem to look on Eastern Europe as spoils of war, with chauvinistic and insulting remarks, for which I must apologize to the peoples of Eastern Europe.

It is high time to understand that neither socialism, nor friendship, nor good-neighbourly relations, nor respect can be built on a foundation of bayonets, tanks, and blood. Relations with any country must be based on taking account of mutual interests, mutual benefit, and the principle of free choice.[20]

Shevardnadze managed to fight off his critics, but characteristically did not even seek to be re-elected to the CPSU Central Committee; having been made a member of the Presidential Council and remaining at the head of the Foreign Ministry until his dramatic resignation in December 1990, his fate reflected the shift in power at the apex of the Soviet pyramid, as well as the malaise in Communist Party circles increased by the East European events.

The Soviet view of the remaining 'fraternal countries' was no less confusing. Presumably all – from China to Yugoslavia, from Albania to Cuba, from North Korea to Laos – were now acknowledged to be socialist (though what this meant was another question; as Nikolai Shishlin remarked, 'You know, we wonder whether we ourselves are a socialist state'[21]). But by what criteria that determination was made – and whether it any longer mattered – was left unclear. For those planning to sort out Soviet concepts and perspectives, on ruling as well as non-ruling communist parties, a lot of work remained to be done.

DISORIENTATION: ORGANIZATIONAL COSTS

Compared to the general propositions of the New Political Thinking, official Moscow showed far greater disarray and defensiveness with regard to the communist world. If previously the growth of the Soviet bloc had been proclaimed inevitable, now its collapse was, a bit shamefacedly, presented as equally inevitable.[22] As for the 'fraternal' parties elsewhere in the world, the Soviet establishment seemed to be giving them less thought, attention, or resources than ever before.

The clearest expression of this unprecedented sense of failure and depression concerning world communism was to be found in the area of 'organizational consequences'. In the spring of 1990 the one 'international' Soviet-sponsored publication aimed at all foreign communist parties, *Problems of Peace and Socialism* (also published in English as *World Marxist Review*) ceased publication.[23] The monthly

journal sponsored by the Institute on the International Labour Movement, *Rabochiy klass i sovremennyy mir* (The Working Class and the
Contemporary World), was about to become a political-science journal under the title, *Polis*, presumably as part of the general scramble
by those who had taught or propagated Marxism-Leninism now to
find legitimacy in the newly-sanctioned field of 'politology'.

Of the institutions attached to the CPSU Central Committee, the
Institute of Social Science (*Institut Obshchestvennykh Nauk*), whose
major function had been the training of communists from abroad,
was about to terminate this activity. Its rector (Yuri Krasin) and
pro-rector (Aleksandr Galkin) sought to find new research tasks for
themselves or else to shift to the training of non-communists. The
USSR Academy of Sciences' Institute on the International Labour
Movement, under Timur Timofeev, faced an uncertain future, as it
was devoting substantial efforts to domestic social problems. Meanwhile the Institute on Socialist Economic Systems, which had dealt
most heavily – and most seriously – with Eastern Europe (under the
direction of Academician Oleg Bogomolov), sought to redefine its
task in geographic rather than ideological terms.

All these were part of an effort within the Social Science Division
of the Academy of Sciences to reconsider the priorities, the organization, and the funding of relevant research, caught as they were (as so
much else in the Soviet Union was) between traditionalists and
innovators, amidst bureaucratic in-fighting and a budget crunch.[24]

FROM 1917 TO 1990

At the time of the October Revolution, Lenin had described world
revolution as 'essential' for the survival of the Soviet state. Three
generations later, there was not a word of protest or excitement
when, in a discussion of a new flag in the RSFSR Supreme Soviet, a
woman deputy (an editor of *Molodaya Gvardiya*) declared on 22 May
1990, 'The formula, "Workers of the World, Unite" on our flag has
long been – you will agree – an absurdity'.

An outside observer might describe the process that had intervened as a slow though characteristic response to cognitive dissonance 'when prophecy fails' (to borrow the title of a familiar
monograph). Another way to characterize it would be to think of it as
a protracted learning process in which ideological axioms and im-
peratives are gradually overridden by a perceived need for realism.

In either case, the expectation of world revolution is either abandoned or else removed into so distant a future as to lose all operational significance. Similarly, belief in the inevitability of the victorious march of the 'working class movement' through history is either tacitly cast aside or else so attenuated as to become a (shaky) article of faith that requires neither validation nor individual exertion.

Thus, while Soviet analysts had managed to face the real world of diplomacy and international security with a well-ordered (though at times improvized) system of precepts, the vision of world revolution had been all but eroded, the future of world communism proved strikingly fuzzy, and – amidst unprecedented candour in the atmosphere of *glasnost'* – a virtual lack of new concepts characterized the Soviet approach to *fin de siècle* communism.

Notes

* I am very grateful for the residency provided by the Rockefeller Foundation at its Study and Conference Center at Bellagio, Italy, in order to draft this chapter. Research for it was also supported by the National Council for Soviet and East European Research and by the International Research and Exchanges Board (with funds from NEH and USIA). None of these organizations is responsible for the views expressed here.

1. O. V. Borisov, 'Soyuz novogo tipa', *Voprosy istorii KPSS*, no. 4, 1984, pp. 34–49; O. Vladimirov, 'Vedushchii faktor mirovogo revolyutsionnogo protsessa', *Pravda*, 21 June 1985. See also I. M. Krivoguz, 'Strategiya i taktika kompartii stran srednego urovnya razvitiya kapitalizma', *Rabochii klass i sovremennyi mir*, no. 5, 1985, pp. 143–57; and *MEMO*, nos. 4 and 5, 1985.
2. 'Revisionism' and 'nationalism' have of course been terms of opprobrium in international communist rhetoric.
3. Aleksandr Bovin, 'Perestroyka i sud'by sotsializma', *Izvestiia*, 11 July 1987. See also Yevgeniy Plimak, 'Novoe myshlenie i perspektivy sotsial'nogo obnovleniya mira', *Voprosy filosofii*, no. 6, 1987:

    Even relatively recently, communists believed that the twentieth century would be the century of the worldwide triumph of socialism. Now, however, it is clear that – no matter how great the natural desire of revolutionaries to bring nearer the hour of victory, this goal is receding into the distant future. The truth is that we underestimated the ability of capitalism to adapt to new conditions, . . . and at the same time we overestimated the speed with which the influence of socialism might spread.

4. German Diligensky, 'Revolyutsionnaya teoriya i sovremennost'',

MEMO, no. 3, 1988, pp. 15–25; English translation also in Steve Hirsch (ed.), *MEMO* (Washington, D.C.: BNA, 1989), pp. 30–45. Another paper by Diligensky is his 'Theory of Revolution Today', in Institute of World History, USSR Academy of Sciences, *Revolutions and Reforms in World History* (Moscow: Nauka, 1990), pp. 236–53. On the same general topic, see also interview with Vladlen Sirotkin, Professor at the Diplomatic Academy of the Foreign Ministry, 'Revolyutsiya v soznanii', in *XX vek i mir*, no. 7, 1988, pp. 17–24; also Sirotkin in Yuri Afanas'ev and Marc Ferro (eds), *50/50: Opyt slovarya novogo myshleniya* (Moscow: Progress, 1989), pp. 70–2, 86–9.

5. *Dialog*, no. 3, 1990, pp. 91–8, with the participation of Vadim Zagladin, Yuri Krasin, Aleksandr Galkin *et al*.

6. This and the following paragraphs are based on the sources cited in the preceding footnotes as well as some forty interviews conducted by the author in Moscow in April and May 1990. There are few other Western analyses of this subject. See, however, Steven Kull, 'Dateline Moscow: Burying Lenin', *Foreign Policy*, no. 78, Spring 1990, pp. 172–91.

7. Yu. Kuznets, in 'Novoe myshlenie v mezhdunarodnykh delakh: kruglyi stol . . .', *Kommunist*, no. 8, 1989, p. 100.

8. *Dialog*, no. 3, 1990, pp. 91–8.

9. Yuri Krasin, 'Towards a new vision of socialism', in Global Research Institute, Institut Obshchestvennykh Nauk pri TsK KPSS, *The Phenomenon of Socialism: Essence, Regularities, Perspectives*, English edn (Moscow, 1990), p. 8. Krasin has been Director of the Institute of Social Science attached to the CPSU Central Committee, the principal training programme for foreign communists.

10. For an 'authoritative' version of this position, see Igor' Pantin and Yevgeniy Plimak, 'Idei K. Marksa na perelome chelovecheskoi tsivilizatsii', *Kommunist*, no. 4, 1990, pp. 28–45.

11. On the latter point, see, for instance, Georgiy Shakhnazarov, 'Vostok – Zapad: k voprosu o deideologizatsii mezhgosudarstvennykh otnoshenii', *Kommunist*, no. 3, 1989, pp. 67–78; Igor' Malashenko, 'Interesy strany: mnimye i real'nye', *Kommunist*, no. 13, 1989, pp. 114–23; Yevgeniy Stepanov, 'Ponyatie "interesy" vo vneshnei politike', *Problemy dal'nego vostoka*, no. 3, 1990, pp. 63–72.

12. For earlier Soviet approaches to Eastern Europe, see, for example, Sarah Terry (ed.), *Soviet Policy in Eastern Europe* (New Haven: Yale University Press, 1984); Zbigniew Brzezinski, *The Soviet Bloc*, rev. edn (Cambridge, MA: Harvard University Press, 1967); also Margot Light, *The Soviet Theory of International Relations* (Brighton: Wheatsheaf, 1988), pp. 145ff., 305ff. For a detailed account of the changing Soviet policy, see Karen Dawisha, *Eastern Europe, Gorbachev, and Reform: The Great Challenge*, 2nd edn (Cambridge University Press, 1990).

13. Alexander Kapto, 'Priority will be given to our Relations with Socialist Countries' (summary of a conference at the Ministry of Foreign Affairs), *International Affairs*, English edn, November 1988, p. 29.

14. Deputy Foreign Minister Ivan Aboimov, 'Development of USSR Relations with the Socialist Countries', *International Affairs*, English edn, October 1988, pp. 38–9.

15. *International Affairs*, English edn, March 1990, pp. 33–4. See also Diligensky, 'Revolyutsionnaya teoriya i sovremennost'', *MEMO*, no. 3, 1988, pp. 23–5.
16. See, for example, Andranik Migranyan, 'An Epitaph to the Brezhnev Doctrine', *Moscow News*, no. 34, 1989, p. 6; and Yevgeniy Ambartsumov, *La Repubblica* (Rome), interview, 13–14 August 1989.
17. Vladimir Lukin, '1989: The Crossroads of History', *Moscow News*, no. 52, 1989, p. 3. See also Yevgeniy Ambartsumov, 'Not Agony but Turn to Life', *Moscow News*, no. 45, 1989, p. 7. For an interesting discussion of the East European experience and its possible lessons for the Soviet Union, see 'Ternistyi put' k politicheskomu plyuralizmu: problemy, konflikty, perspektivy', in *Voprosy istorii KPSS*, no. 8, August 1990, pp. 15–25.
18. Yevgeniy Shashkov, 'Vostochnaya Evropa – vospominaniya i realii', *Kommunist*, no. 10, 1990, pp. 113–19. See also Valeriy Musatov, 'Peremeny v Vostochnoi Evrope i nasha perestroyka', *Pravda*, 14 May 1990. Musatov was Deputy Chief of the International Department of the CPSU Central Committee.
19. *International Herald Tribune*, 27 June 1990.
20. *Pravda*, 26 June 1990. For the charges and Shevardnadze's replies, see also *Sovetskaia Rossiia*, 22 June 1990; *Pravda*, 5 and 11 July 1990; USSR Ministry of Foreign Affairs, *Vestnik*, no. 13 (71) and no. 14 (72), 15 and 31 July 1990. See also Shevardnadze's interview in *Argumenty i fakty*, no. 2, 1990, p. 2.
21. Paris *Libération*, 11 September 1989, p. 4.
22. The new political parties and fronts (other than the CPSU) emerging in the Soviet Union have been singularly lacking in interest in the communist world beyond the USSR, except for an occasional barbed comment about Cuba and North Korea.
23. The journal had been established in 1958, appeared as a monthly in a number of languages, and had had its editorial offices in Prague. Its internal politics, and the experience of its Soviet staff members, present an interesting topic that remains to be studied.
24. The International Department of the CPSU Central Committee continued to handle the extensive contacts with foreign communist parties. But there was a growing sense in official circles in Moscow that somehow these contacts did not matter as much as they had earlier on. Indeed, while previously it had been important which of several rival communist parties or factions in a given country (for instance, Finland, India, Japan, Greece, or Spain) Moscow was prepared to deal with and in effect recognize as the legitimate one, it had become the tendency under Gorbachev to deal with all such groups, in the novel spirit of ecumenical diversity. On its background and activities, see Vernon V. Aspaturian, *The Role of the International Department in the Soviet Foreign Policy Process* (Washington: Foreign Service Institute, 1989).

7 Some Concluding Observations

T. H. Rigby

It was new ways of thinking about Russia's and the world's problems, and the paths to their resolution, that ushered in the bureaucratic dictatorship of the Soviet Communist Party, with all its fateful domestic and international consequences, and now it is new ways of thinking about these matters that is ushering it out. In both cases, moreover, the new ways of thinking were personified in a 'transformational' leadership,[1] operating in a context of mounting socio-economic and political crisis, and offering a path away from poverty, backwardness, tyranny, obscurantism and war.

One should not overdraw the parallels. Lenin's revolution was Russia's only successful revolution from below so far, and his thinking was thus shared with and implemented through a new, revolutionary political elite. Gorbachev's, by contrast, is more a revolution from above, of which there are several partial parallels in Russian history, and his thinking has thus been shared with, and implemented through, elements within the old elites.[2] Lenin's thinking impelled him and his followers, for the ultimate sake of that communist society that could alone provide genuine human freedom, peace and well-being, to subject all existing individual and group autonomies to their political will, incorporating all spheres of social activity into a single organizational structure integrated by the party apparatus, and deploying massive coercion to prevent any non-official public communication, association or assembly, while conducting relationships with the bourgeois world on the assumption that their underlying reality was one of zero-sum conflict. Gorbachev's thinking led him, by contrast, to see freedom, peace and well-being as requiring a *restoration* of individual and group autonomies, the emancipation of most spheres of social activity from centralized administrative direction, the tolerance of non-official public communication, association and assembly, and the attainment of accommodations with the bourgeois world, since common dangers had become more fundamental than the sources of mutual conflict.

Consequently, despite important shared elements in the revolutionary thrust of Lenin's and Gorbachev's new thinking, the practical measures that flowed from them were almost the mirror-image of each other. To put it so baldly may seem an injustice to Lenin. What about the *re*thinking embodied in his NEP and his deeds and writings in the final months of his active political life? And indeed, despite the partial and unsystematic character of this rethinking, it at least suggests that, had Lenin remained at the helm for a few more years, he *might* have steered Russia decisively towards a different form of society from the mono-organizational socialism which had begun to take shape during the Civil War and which was to triumph completely in the 1930s. Whatever his unrealized intentions, however, it was Lenin's earlier thinking and actions that had laid the foundations of the mono-organizational system, and two generations had to suffer the consequences of these 'mistakes' before they began to be 'corrected'.

It was only in the late 1980s that Gorbachev and his allies and supporters moved openly to repudiate the essentials of that system, characterizing it by such terms as the 'administrative-command system', 'bureaucratic autocracy', and even 'totalitarianism'. And it was to be 1990 before this way of thinking was matched by decisive action: the abdication by the party apparatus of its 'leading and directing' authority over all legitimate social institutions, both official and non-official. It was this authority that had made the system a *mono*-organizational one, and its abandonment was the fundamental condition for discarding such other basic components of the system as the monopoly over every sphere of activity by officially designated agencies, the command economy, the ban on alternative parties and intra-CPSU factions, the political management of information, and the ideologization of education and culture.

Nevertheless, as the preceding chapters make clear, the new thinking that led to this revolutionary change did not, of course, start with Gorbachev. Its roots, in fact, go right back to the death of Stalin in 1953, when his heirs were forced to do some thinking of their own, in order to safeguard the essentials of the system while effecting a transition from tyrannical to oligarchical rule, seeking to modernize dangerously backward areas of Soviet life, and to lessen internal and external pressures while these delicate changes were under way. The main elements in the resultant within-system *perestroika* were the de-deification of Stalin, the curbing of the arbitrary powers of the political police, the reduced demonization of, and isolation from, the capitalist West, the partial de-ideologization of areas of intellectual

life, a new emphasis on satisfying material needs as a source of mass
support, and the move to (competitive) 'peaceful coexistence' in
East–West relations.

These measures proved fairly successful for their immediate purposes and they stabilized the mono-organizational system in a modi-
fied form that persisted for over three decades. However, they also
had unintended effects of fateful consequence. They perforated the
'iron curtain' and dissolved the fear-engendered 'atomization' of the
population. They fostered doubt and cynicism about official doctrines, values and symbols, while affording access, though often
difficult and dangerous, to alternatives. It now became easier not
only to think independently, but also to share one's thoughts within a
revitalized private sphere of family and friends, both verbally and
increasingly in written form as well. A many-faceted 'counter-
culture' emerged, one facet of which was oriented towards political
issues. Where it assumed an organized form the KGB would go into
action, but it was no longer possible to nip all wrong-thinking in the
bud or to prevent substantial sections of the population from becoming aware of it. The few thousands of active dissidents were therefore
just the most visible part of a freely thinking (and talking) public
(*obshchestvennost'*) running into the millions. There were innumerable personal linkages between this public and the nation's various
elites, and a heavy overlap with the main body of the intelligentsia,
including (and perhaps especially) those employed in the various
policy-oriented 'think-tanks' that came to the fore under Brezhnev.[3]

All this was a necessary prerequisite to what has happened under
Gorbachev. On the one hand there was an urgent need for new ideas
for reforming Soviet society, and where were these to come from if
not from more original and independent-minded elements within the
official think-tanks? Small wonder that Gorbachev was to draw many
of these people into his entourage, some of whom passed into
positions of great power and influence, as Archie Brown has shown.
On the other hand, the relaxation after 1986 of controls over information and public expression, association and assembly would scarcely
have released such a massive explosion of political activity in the
following years had this not been gestating for a generation in the
submerged counter-culture. Its effect was to produce a rapidly
changing and ever more sophisticated and varied context of publicly
expressed knowledge, ideas and values within which the thinking of
top policymakers developed. The 'New Thinking' of 1985–6 soon lost
its freshness and this cognitive dissonance was as essential a factor as

objective conditions in engendering the process of radicalization observable in all the policy areas we have studied.

Our examination of the origins and trajectories of recent Soviet thinking in the four areas of politics, economics, foreign relations and inter-ethnic relations has revealed, however, some significant differences. Thus, while they all experienced a 'prehistory' in the Khrushchev and Brezhnev years, involving a growing if still limited *de facto* pluralism of ideas, access to Western scholarly literature, and (largely covert) 'debates', this process is shown by Professors Brown and Dallin to have been a substantially cumulative one in the case of domestic and foreign politics, while in economics, as noted by Professor Nove, it was largely a matter of exploring false panaceas for the centrally planned economy, and in inter-ethnic relations, as Professor Lapidus points out, the official shibboleths were zealously shielded from the potentially demythologizing concepts and research findings of ethnographers and sociologists. Rather similar patterns are apparent in the Gorbachev era itself. Within a year or so the new *political* thinking was not only beginning to be voiced publicly but also to find expression in official policies and practices, and then, gaining reinforcement from positive domestic and foreign responses, it advanced step by step to transform by 1990 both the Soviet political order and the role of the USSR in the world system of states. In the economic sphere, by contrast, while public criticism of the 'command' system became ever more open and radical from 1987 onwards, commensurate reforms were not initiated until 1990, by which time the deterioration in economic performance had reached critical levels. In inter-ethnic relations the pattern is different again: the under-estimation of ethnic nationalism and consequent lack of adequate thought given to the possible side-effects of relaxing political controls, led to a series of improvized responses to unanticipated crises, so that actual change far outran thought-out policy.

I turn now to a number of conceptual and analytical points. First, it is worth asking whether the scope of this book does not involve too loose a usage of the term 'New Thinking' itself. It was at first, indeed, applied mostly to new Soviet understandings of world politics, and some writers, both in the Soviet Union and abroad, still prefer to limit its use in that way. For example, even the authors of the 1990 edition of the standard handbook for party 'activists' (approved for printing in August 1989) confine their discussion of 'New Political Thinking' exclusively to questions of Soviet foreign policy.[4] Analogously, *perestroika* is often identified exclusively with economic policy, *glasnost'* with information policy, and democratization with political institutions. This looks very much like a vestige of the 'old thinking' according to which each policy area in the Soviet Union is, or should be, legitimated by (or deduced from) specific doctrinal formulations closely integrated into basic propositions of Marxist-Leninist theory. Obviously, it does not sit well with the content or indeed the very title of Gorbachev's *Perestroika: New Thinking for our Country and the World*. It is clear that for him and for those close to him, 'New Thinking', *perestroika, glasnost'* and 'democratization' should all figure in the transformation process in every field of policy.

Our account raises some difficult questions regarding the relationships between thought, word and action, the dynamics of which have changed so profoundly between 1985 and 1990. In interpreting the spoken and written word, moreover, we must bear in mind the different audiences addressed (for example, the Politburo, bureaucratic elites, educated public opinion, the masses, foreign governments and publics and so on) as well as the possibility of 'hidden agendas'. And here we should note that it is not only Gorbachev and other top leaders whose public writings and utterances may conceal their long-term or even shorter-term goals: all Soviet officials and intellectuals, including those offering advice to leaders, are habituated to a system where such concealments may be essential to the achievement, step by step, of any serious change. The question of questions regarding 'hidden agendas' is – to put the alternatives in their most extreme form – whether Gorbachev was aiming from the beginning at what he achieved only in 1990, namely the abolition of the CPSU's constitutional monopoly and the transfer of supreme power from the Politburo to a newly-established Presidency, or whether these resulted from a series of pragmatic reactions to the unintended consequences of measures with far more limited goals?[5] Most specialists would perhaps offer a more complicated hypothesis about the development of Gorbachev's intentions than either of these polar opposites, but the point is that, like most problems of identifying the original 'agenda' in a complex and dynamic sequence of events, the kind of evidence required to solve it definitively is not yet available and perhaps never will be, even if future memoirs and archival access may lighten our ignorance.

The discernment of motives and perceptions is no less encumbered with the problem of dissimulation and the tactical use of ideas than is the discernment of intentions. The 'classical' question here is what prompted the predominantly conservative Soviet leadership of the mid-1980s to opt for a radical *perestroika* in the first place. Few would contest that the most important factor was the rapidly declining effectiveness of the Soviet economic system, and this was certainly a *necessary* condition for *perestroika*; but was it a *sufficient* condition? Why did they not persist with the alternative strategy of battening down the hatches and tightening discipline and belts in a resurgent 'barracks socialism', which was the thrust of their policies under Andropov and in the first year of Gorbachev's incumbency? The answer surely lies in changing perceptions of the nature and depth of the country's problems and of the feasibility and likely effectiveness of different remedies. The influence of such intellectuals as Zaslav-skaya, Aganbegyan, Butenko and others in *changing* those percep-tions, and first and foremost those of Gorbachev, must therefore be seen as another necessary (though not sufficient) condition of the shift to systemic reform. On so much the authors of this book are unanimous, but we are also aware that these conditions were not immediately translatable into policy measures but had to be mediated through the interpersonal dynamics of the top leaders and their senior officials and advisors – the classical 'black box' – and here wisdom begins with acknowledging our ignorance.

This applies in no less measure to the hotly debated subsidiary question of the weight of military considerations in motivating the New Political Thinking, and specifically whether the strong NATO response to the Soviet military build-up of the 1970s, culminating in President Reagan's Strategic Defence Initiative, by raising the stakes of military competition beyond the capacity of the Soviet economy to match, did not deliver the *coup de grâce* to the 'old thinking'. Here we can perhaps at least agree that the New Political Thinking was not *merely* a cynically pragmatic ploy to gain time for the Soviet Union to prepare a military come-back and that a serious attempt to re-evaluate world changes from a Marxist-Leninist perspective was involved.[6] But 'unpacking' this proposition to reveal the 'real' per-ceptions, motives and intentions of various individual and collective participants in dynamic interplay over a several-year period is surely beyond our capacities, however worthwhile the by-products of at-tempting it might prove. The researcher faces the same difficulty in all policy areas, and although the emergence from 1989 of an openly pluralistic and increasingly vigorous public political process should mitigate it, many large issues of interpretation are likely to remain unresolvable.

The points made in the last four paragraphs may seem banal to some readers, but they are surprisingly often neglected, and they also help to set the agenda for further research. There are two further dimensions of Soviet new thinking which likewise call for closer study and which deserve mention here.

The first is political semantics. The propagation of such 'buzz-words' as *glasnost'*, 'law-bound state' (*pravovoe gosudarstvo*), 'administrative-command system' (*komandno-administrativnaya sistema*), 'humane socialism' (*gumannyy sotsializm*), and so on, has had a major role in helping to restructure perceptions and attitudes. The thrust of most of these terms will be familiar, but one calls for specific comment. The year 1988 saw the emergence of the phrase 'administrative-command *methods*', its speedy adoption by Gorbachev himself, and then its extention to characterize the whole traditional Soviet socio-political order as an 'administrative-command *system*'. The latter's connotation seems identical with that of my preferred term for the system, 'mono-organizational socialism', namely the running of every sphere of life through a designated hierarchy of bureaucratic command, the whole being directed, supervised and co-ordinated by the command-hierarchy of the Communist Party. This pejorative labelling of the fundamental structuring principle of the existing order was the first unambiguous signal that Gorbachev was resolved to move from restructuring *within* the system to restructuring *of* the system, and its implications struck at the hallowed 'leading and directing' role of the Party.

In addition to such highly-charged programmatic terms, the Gorbachev years have seen an accelerating turnover in everyday political vocabulary, as words compromised by association with the practices of the 'administrative-command system' are replaced by others often adopted from abroad. For example in many contexts the standard Russian word for 'leader', *rukovoditel'*, has been largely supplanted by *lider*, a word long ago borrowed from English but used in the past mostly in certain specific non-political contexts. The Soviet head of state is no longer a *predsedatel'*, but a *prezident* – although the essential meaning of both words is identical. The federal legislative body, the Supreme Soviet (*Verkhovnyy Sovet SSSR*), along with its equivalents in the republics, is now frequently called the Soviet *parlament*, a term largely restricted in the past to foreign propaganda usage – and is intended to gain in dignity thereby. Such semantic shifts cannot be dismissed as simply the latest tarting up of the façade, for they correlate with profound changes in the roles of particular posts and institutions. A further aspect is the new political loading carried by certain ostensibly neutral terms. Examples are the words 'normal' (*normal'nyy*) and 'civilized' (*tsivilizovannyy*) when applied to practices and conditions *not* found in the USSR, and most tellingly in the phrase 'in the civilized countries'.

We see then that the political semantics of the Gorbachev era offer a rich – and largely untouched – field of research. The same can be said of the final component of new Soviet ways of thinking which I wish to mention, namely its value component. The new-won freedom of expression in combination with the deepening revulsion from 'real socialism' have proved a deadly solvent of such official values of the 'administrative-command system' as *partiynost* (party-spiritedness), *printsipial'nost* (adherence to principle) and *edinodushie* (unanimity), and so on. The values that have now come to the fore are not limited to such obvious ones as freedom, justice and truth. For example, 'common sense' (*zdravyy smysl*) has emerged as one of the most desirable personal and social attributes in the lexicon of many politicians, journalists and scholars. A very important aspect is the reassertion of submerged ethnically-linked values and their accompanying symbols, as we saw in Professor Lapidus' chapter. There is a deeper level too. Many Soviet people in all areas of society perceive a crying need for a spiritual renovation and not just a political and economic one. The mendacity, hate, slavishness and heartlessness engendered by Marxism-Leninism in action are seen as having left the country a moral and spiritual wasteland. The first prophets of spiritual renewal were of course to be found among the suffering 'dissidents' of the pre-Gorbachev generation, from the Sakharovs and Solzhenitsyns down to the simple Baptist carpenter unwilling to deny his faith, and their influence on the perceptions and values of the Soviet intellectual elite on the eve of *perestroika* should not be ignored. But it was the new freedom of expression after 1986 that converted such perceptions and attitudes into a mass moral-political force. Historians, sociologists, journalists, film-makers and writers held up a mirror to the spiritual face of the Soviet people and the reaction was distress, catharsis, and moral revulsion. It is significant that ordinary Soviet discourse offered no language to identify the precious qualities now seen as lost and these were drawn perforce from the deeper Christian levels of the national culture. Two concepts have proved particularly potent: *pokayanie* (repentance) and *miloserdie* (*caritas*: mercy or charity). These are matters that we cannot explore in detail in this book,[7] but future scholarship must give serious attention to the interplay between the cognitive-instrumental and moral-spiritual components in the new thinking that has transformed the Soviet Union under Gorbachev.

Notes

1. See Noel M. Tichy and Mary A. Devanna, *The Transformational Leader* (New York: Wiley, 1986).
2. See T. H. Rigby, *The Changing Soviet System. Mono-organisational Socialism from its Origins to Gorbachev's Perestroika* (Aldershot: Elgar, 1990), chapters 8 and 9.
3. Further on the 'counter-(or second) culture' and its significance, see Geoffrey Hosking, *The Awakening of the Soviet Union* (Cambridge, Mass.: Harvard University Press, 1990), chapter 4; and T. H. Rigby, 'Mono-organisational Socialism and the Civil Society', in David W. Lovell and Chandran Kukathas, *The Transition from Socialism: State and Civil Society in Gorbachev's USSR* (London: Longman, 1991).
4. S. V. Kolesnikov *et al., Knizhka partiynogo aktivista: 1990* (Moscow: Politizdat, 1990), pp. 201–12.
5. A maximalist view of Gorbachev's concealed intentions is offered by John Gooding in his 'Gorbachev and Democracy', *Soviet Studies*, vol. 42 (April 1990), no. 2.
6. This point is emphasized from differing perspectives in Robert F. Miller, *Soviet Foreign Policy Today* (Sydney: Allen & Unwin, 1991), chapter 1; V. Kubalkova and A. A. Cruickshank, *Thinking about Soviet New Thinking* (Berkeley: Institute of International Studies, University of California, 1989); and Boris Meissner, '"New Thinking" and Soviet Foreign Policy', *Aussenpolitik*, no. 11, 1989, pp. 101–18. On the specific influence of military-strategic rethinking, see Michael MccGwire, *Perestroika and Soviet National Security* (Washington: The Brookings Institution, 1990).
7. For an excellent survey, see Tamara V. Samsonova, *Perestrojka der Ethik und Ethik der Perestrojka* (Cologne: Federal Institute of East-European and International Studies, Report no. 30, 1990).

Index

Abalkin, L.I.   34, 36, 67
Aboimov, Ivan   100
Adamishin, A.   24, 28
'administrative-command
    system'   108, 109
Afanas'ev, Yu.N.   4, 10, 67, 100
Aganbegyan, A.G.   20, 30, 107
Albright, David   84
Alekseev, S.S.   2, 9
Alma Ata demonstrations   45, 47,
    57, 66, 69
Ambartsumov, Ye.A.   101
American Civil War   65
Andropov, Yu.V.   42, 43, 56, 107
Antonov, Mikhail   36
Armenia   17, 58–9
Arutyunov, Sergey   67
Arutyunyan, U.V.   65
Aspaturian, Vernon V.   101
Atkinson, Scott R.   85

Bagramov, Eduard   47
Ball, Terence   9
Baltic republics   16, 28, 48, 51, 62
    (see also Estonia, Latvia,
    Lithuania)
Bazarov, V.A.   29
Beissinger, Mark   66
Berdyaev, Nikolay   3
Berliner, Joseph   36
Bialer, Seweryn   66, 75, 83
Bogomolov, O.T.   35, 79, 98
Bolshevism   37
Borisov, O.V.   99
Bovin, A.Ye.   79, 87, 90, 99
Brezhnev, L.I.   1, 3, 42, 44, 56
    doctrine   95
    era   1, 3, 8, 12, 13, 14, 15, 16,
        40, 41, 42, 43, 49, 52, 54,
        104, 105
Bromley, Yu.V.   41, 65
Brown, Archie   ix, 1, 8, 12, 26,
    27, 104, 105
Brumberg, Abraham   84

Brzezinski, Zbigniew   100
Burlatsky, F.M.   1, 9, 13, 14, 26,
    27, 79, 82
Butenko, A.P.   10, 107
Butler, W.E.   84

Chayanov, A.V.   29
checks and balances   20, 21
Chernenko, K.U.   7, 14, 26
Chernobyl'   57
China   14, 31, 76, 81, 87, 96, 97
civil society   17, 19
Civil War   103
Committee for the Supervision of
    the Constitution see
    Constitution
commodity–money relations   30
commodity production   33
Communist Party of the Soviet
    Union   4, 8, 13, 19, 20, 22,
        38, 48, 49, 63, 78, 82, 97, 101,
        102, 106, 108
    Central Committee   4, 6, 13, 16,
        18, 20, 26, 58, 59, 62, 66, 67,
        70, 80, 97, 98, 101
        plenums   9, 34, 47, 57,
            59, 70
    Conferences   59
    Congresses
        of RSFSR party   19, 81, 96
        of USSR, Twenty-Eighth   6,
            9, 11, 17, 19, 21, 44, 45, 96
        Twenty-Seventh   56
    of Estonia   67
    General Secretary   21, 23
    'leading role'   18, 20, 28
    Politburo   6, 45, 78, 82, 106
    of Russia   6, 49, 96
Confederation of
    Anarcho-Syndicalists   36
Congress of People's Deputies of
    the USSR   17, 18, 26
Constitution, Committee for the
    Supervision of   2, 21, 26

Constitution – *continued*
  of the USSR 13, 18, 70, 92
  of the Russian republic 22
Cooperators, All-Union Society
  of 35
Council of the Federation 63
Council of Ministers 20
Crow, Suzanne 85
Cruickshank, A.A. 83, 84, 85,
  110
Csaba, Laszlo 36

Dadayan, V. 36
Dallin, Alexander vii, ix, 8, 66,
  71, 86, 105
Dawisha, Karen 100
Democratic Russia 4, 6
democratic capitalism 7
democratic socialism 7, 17
Democratic Union 36
Devanna, Mary A. 110
Deytsev, S.E. 28
Diligensky, G.G. 88, 99, 100, 101
Dostoevsky, F.M. 36
Drobizheva, L.M. 65
Dyachenko, V. 29
Dzarasov, S. 32

elections 2, 48
Engels, Friedrich 31, 33
Estonia 51, 57
Etkind, A.M. 27
Evangelista, Matthew 84
Evans, Jr., Alfred B. 9

Fal'kner, S. 29
Farr, James 3, 9
Fedoseev, P.N. 15
Ferro, Marc 100
'Five Hundred Days Plan' 63
Friedman, Milton 35
Fukuyama, Francis 84

Gaidar, E. 34, 35
Galkin, Aleksandr 98, 100
Garthoff, Raymond 84
Georgia 17
glasnost' 2, 8, 9, 15, 31, 39, 45,
  46, 47, 48, 49, 50, 57, 58, 75,

77, 87, 99, 106, 108
Glavlit 16
Golan, Galia 85
Gooding, John 110
Gorbachev, M.S. 3, 8, 9, 18, 20,
  46, 47, 60, 63, 68, 71, 82, 93,
  95, 96, 108, 109, 110
  accession to General Secretary-
    ship 4, 26, 39, 40, 55, 72
  and foreign policy 4, 8, 74, 76,
    77, 80, 81
  and *glasnost'* 12
  and nationality problem 7, 39,
    43, 44, 45, 47, 51, 53, 54,
    55, 57, 58, 59, 60, 62, 64,
    68, 69, 96
  and *perestroika* 1, 10, 58, 61,
    70, 106, 108
  and pluralism 7, 19, 23, 24
  and reform, economic 63, 64
  and reform, political 21, 23,
    39, 46, 49, 62, 63, 69, 102
  leadership 13, 43, 44, 53, 57,
    78, 81, 86, 104, 105, 107
  New Thinking 2, 4, 6, 9, 10, 14,
    16, 17, 20, 23, 27, 55, 56, 102,
    103, 106
Gosplan 93
Gozman, L.Ya. 27
Groman, V.G. 29
Grossman, V.S. 34
Gruyter, Aldine de 84
gumannyy sotsializm ('humane
  socialism') 108

Hallik, K. 67
Hanson, Russell L. 9
Harding, Neil 26
Hasegawa, Tsuyoshi 84
Hayek, F. von 35
Hill, Ronald J. 26
Hirsch, Steve 100
Hodnett, Grey 65
Hoffmann, Erik 66
Holloway, David 73, 84
Hosking, Geoffrey 110
Hough, Jerry 85
Howard, Roy 92
Hungary 37

Il'in, Aleksey 6
Izyumov, A. 85

Juviler, Peter 84

Kachanov, V.E. 10
Kagalovsky, K. 34
Kalensky, V.G. 14, 20, 27, 28
Kantorovich, L.V. 29
Kapto, Alexander 100
Katyn massacre 94
Kerimov, D.A. 10
KGB 4, 6, 20, 66, 104
Khanin, V. 31, 32
Khrushchev, N.S. 3
   era 77, 79, 82, 105
Kimura, Hiroshi 84
Kirgiz Writers' Union 67
Kiselev, V. 38
Kobo, Kh. 10
Kolbin, G.V. 45
Kolesnikov, S.V. 110
*komandno-administrativnaya
   sistema see* 'administrative-
   command system'
Komsomol 66
Kondratev, N.D. 29
Kornai, J. 35
Kortunov, Andrey 84, 85
Kosolapov, R.I. 42, 43, 66
Kozlov, V. 65
Krasin, Yu.A. 98, 100
Krivoguz, I.M. 99
Krupnik, I.I. 41, 66
Kubalkova, Vendulka 83, 84, 85,
   110
Kukathas, Chandran 110
Kull, Steven 100
Kunaev, D.A. 45
Kunitsyn, G.I. 67
Kurashvili, B.P. 19
Kuznets, Yu. 100

labour market 37
labour-theory of value 29, 30
Lapidus, Gail vii, x, 7, 8, 9, 39,
   66, 105, 109
Latsis, O.R. 35
Latvia 17, 51, 57

Law on Secession 52
Legvold, Robert 83
Lemeshev, M. Ya. 10
Lenin, V.I. 31, 33, 34, 42, 43, 50,
   69, 90, 92, 98, 102, 103
Leninism 13
Leontief, Wassili 29
Liberman, Ye.G. 29
Ligachev, Ye.K. 2, 5, 35, 45, 78,
   80, 82, 96
Light, Margot 83, 100
Lisichkin, Gennadiy 30
Lithuania 17, 49, 51, 54, 62
Lovell, David W. 110
Lukin, Vladimir 95, 100
Lynch, Allen 83

Madison, James 15, 20
Makashov, General Albert 96
Malashenko, Igor' 100
market economy 7, 20, 37
market socialism 35
Marx, Karl 31, 33, 37, 90, 92
Marxism 6, 7, 89, 90, 92, 93
Marxism-Leninism 6, 7, 12, 14,
   17, 25, 26, 32, 33, 48, 73, 75,
   86, 88, 92, 98, 106, 107, 109
Mau, V. 36
McCarthy, Senator Joseph 96
MccGwire, Michael 110
Medvedev, Roy A. 26
Meissner, Boris 84, 110
Melkumyan, M.I. 10
Melville, Andrei (Mel'vil',
   A.Yu.) 9, 24, 28, 78, 85
Meyer, Stephen 84
Migranyan, Andranik 27, 101
Miller, Robert F. 110
mnogovlastie ('many powers') 2
Moldavia 48
Molotov–Ribbentrop Pact 51, 57,
   62, 94
Mukomel', V.I. 27
multi-party system
   (*mnogopartiynost'*) 19
Musatov, Valeriy 101

Nagorno-Karabakh dispute 58,
   59, 62, 64, 67, 69

Nazi–Soviet deal, 1939 *see*
  Molotov–Ribbentrop Pact
Nemchinov, V.S.   30
Nenarokov, A.P.   67
NEP (New Economic Policy)   103
Nikitin, A.I.   78
nomenklatura   33
Notkina, T.A.   10
Nove, Alec   vii, x, 7, 9, 105
Novozhilov, V.V.   29
Nureev, R.   36

October Revolution   93, 98
  seventieth anniversary of   58
Odom, William   85

Pantin, I.   33, 100
Parrott, Bruce   84
Patenaude, Bertrand   66
perestroika   viii, 1, 6, 8, 11, 16, 25,
  31, 37, 39, 46, 52, 54, 55, 58,
  67, 69, 87, 105, 106, 107, 109
Petrakov, N.Ya.   30, 34, 35
Petrovsky, Vladimir   82
Pinsker, B.   35
Piskotin, M.I.   3, 9
Plimak, Ye.   33, 99, 100
Poland   37, 94
Politburo *see* Communist Party
political pluralism   7, 8, 23, 24
Poloz'kov, Ivan   5
Popov, G.Kh.   4, 33, 34, 36, 37,
  38
Popov, P.I.   29
Prague Spring   11, 23
Pravda, Alex   vii
pravovoe gosudarstvo ('law-bound
  state') *see* rule of law
Presidency   20, 106
Presidential Council   82, 97
Primakov, Ye.M.   82
Prokhanov, Aleksandr   36
Prokopenko, A.I.   10
Protashchik, A.A.   10
Pyasheva, L.   35

Rakhmanin, Oleg   86
Reagan, President Ronald   107
regulated market   35

Reysner, L.A.   27
Rigby, T.H.   vii, xi, 102, 110
Roberts, Cynthia   84
Rozman, Gilbert   27
rule of law   17, 108
Rumyantsev, Oleg   22
Ryzhkov, N.I.   20

Sakharov, A.D.   3, 18, 26, 52
samizdat   15
Samsonova, T.V.   110
sblizhenie ('rapprochement')   42
Second World War   51, 54, 67
Selyunin, G.   31, 38
separation of powers   18, 20, 21,
  22
Sergeev, A.   33
Sestanovich, Stephen   85
Shablinsky, I.G.   28
Shakhnazarov, G.Kh.   14, 21, 27,
  82, 100
Shashkov, Yevgeniy   101
Shatalin, S.S.   20, 30, 34, 35, 37
Shenfield, Stephen   84
Shevardnadze, Eduard   4, 8, 71,
  74, 76, 78, 82, 96, 97, 101
Shevtsov, V.S.   13, 26
Sheynis, V.L.   19, 27
Shishlin, Nikolai   97
Shmelev, N.P.   31
Siberian rivers project   44
Šik, Ota   11
Simoniya, N.A.   10, 27
Sirotkin, Vladlen   100
sliyanie ('merger' or 'fusion')   42,
  51, 56
Smoke, Richard   84
Sobchak, A.A.   4
'socialist pluralism'   23, 24
SOFE   30
Soloukhin, V.A.   34
Solzhenitsyn, A.I.   36
Soviet Association of Political
  Sciences   21
Stalin, J.V.   29, 34, 41, 67, 92, 103
  era   23, 29, 59
Stalinism   31, 34, 37, 46, 48
Staravoytova, G.V.   52, 65
State Duma   22

'statisation' (*ogosudarstvlenie*) 17
Stepanov, Yevgeniy 100
Sumgait massacre 59
Supreme Soviet of the RSFSR 2,
  49, 96, 98
Supreme Soviet of the USSR 2,
  14, 17, 26, 51, 61, 68, 69, 81,
  108
Suslov, M.A. 15
Sutela, Pekka 30, 38

Tabata, S. 36
tamizdat 15
Tatu, Michel 66
Tbilisi demonstration 62, 64
Terry, Sarah 100
Thatcher, Margaret 35
'The Third Way' 6, 11, 35
Tichy, Noel M. 110
Tikhonov, Vladimir 35
Timofeev, Timur 98
Tsipko, A.S. 37, 90

Union Treaty, draft of 6, 63
Uzbek Writers' Union 67

Vainshtein, Albert 30
Valjas, Vaino 67
Valkenier, Elizabeth 85
Vilchek, V. 38
Vishnevsky, A.G. 10, 27
Vladimirov, O. 99
Volkov, A.I. 91
Vyshinsky, M.P. 10

Walras, M.E.L. 37
Warsaw Pact 96
Wettig, Gerhard 85
Wishnick, Elizabeth 84
Woodby, Sylvia 9, 84

Yakovlev, A.N. 2, 6, 8, 10, 78, 82
Yaroshenko 29
Yel'tsin, B.N. 2, 4, 20, 22, 49, 63,
  67
Yevstigneev, V. 34
Yurovsky, L. 29

Zagladin, Vadim 100
Zaslavskaya, T.I. 30, 107
Zav'yalova, A.N. 10
Zhurkin, V.V. 94